Being a Christian Husband

Acknowledgements

I would like to thank friends and colleagues but particularly my fellow church members for their helpful advice and encouragement in writing this book. Thanks are also due to David Clark, from Evangelical Press, who kept me on track when I was tempted to give up.

Most of all, I would like to thank my wife Lois, who has made the task of a Christian husband more a delight than a duty.

Foreword

There has been an unprecedented attack on the biblical teaching on marriage in our day. Radical feminist philosophy said that the traditional married family was oppressive. For example, Anthony Giddens (at one time family policy advisor to Tony Blair) has defined the pure relationship as one which either partner can leave at any time. In other words, traditional marriage is wrong and oppressive because the partners have an obligation to stay together. Over the past fifteen or more years government policies have relentlessly undermined the family. But many in the church have attacked biblical teaching on marriage as well. They say that it was culturally conditioned, and that distinctive roles for husbands and wives have no place in the twenty-first century.

Where does this leave Christian husbands? Are they to take a lead in the marriage? If so, they may be accused of sexism, even chauvinism. But if they fail to take a lead, they may be accused of passivity.

This book argues that the answer is not to retreat into traditionalism. The author fully affirms the many advantages and freedoms which women enjoy in our society today. But equally, he shows that to throw out distinctive roles for husbands and wives is to miss out on the beauty of God's design for marriage. He explains that the purpose of marriage is to reflect something of the glory of Christ's relationship with the church. And that relationship is non-reversible! Christ does not lead one day and then let the church lead the next day. But the way that he leads is not selfish or tyrannical; it is for the benefit of the church. Yes, there are all too many husbands who have justified sinful repression by a wrongful use of the Bible's teaching on headship. And wives have suffered from that kind of abuse. But equally, there are many Christian wives who suffer because their husbands are passive, take no initiative, and fail to take responsibility.

The author describes the ways that a Christ-like husband should take responsibility for the well-being of his wife and family. His arguments are faithful to Scripture and relevant to the modern world. My own testimony is that it is not oppressive but joyful and fulfilling to be married to a man who lives out the teaching of Ephesians 5; the teaching that is so attractively set out in the following pages.

In an age of gender confusion in both society and the church, this is a much needed book.

Sharon James

Preface

At the time of writing I have been married over 30 years. In that time life's progression has seen us move from penniless students to relative affluence, from humble jobs to positions of seniority, via several homes and two children. How does a marriage survive so long through so many transitions?

It was more than 10 years before we came to re-examine what it was to have a marriage based on biblical grounds, and this entailed going back to the bible to see what was said there. This re-assessment and our acceptance of the roles outlined there for a husband and wife provided the platform for our marriage and gave it resilience.

I have seen the marriages of friends close to us, and those of many others, not survive those same transitions. Why is it that the failure rate is so high in what is a God given relationship – marriage?

Although there are good Christian books available on marriage, what I began to realise is that what has been lost in many of them is the biblical perspective of distinct roles for the husband and the wife.

You often hear Christian couples saying that ours is a '50/50 marriage'; that we are to 'submit to each other'. Indeed, the Church of England marriage service has the bride and the groom make exactly the same commitment to each other, yet that same service preserves the traditional Christian teaching that marriage is a picture of the relationship between Jesus Christ and his church.[1] The Bible clearly teaches that the responsibilities of Christ and the church differ widely.

If in the marriage the husband is to model himself on the Lord Jesus Christ, and the wife is to see her example in the marriage relationship as being that of the church, then it follows that the roles of husband and wife are different.

What are those differences? What is the distinctive role of the husband? And how can this role be worked out in practice modern Britain?

A superficial glance at the contents of this book might lead some to think I take an old fashioned view of the role of women – regretting the passing of a previous age. But I am glad to be living in this exciting vibrant era. My working life shows that I have a high regard for women and their abilities – I am currently a director of two companies where all my fellow directors are women.

What I say in this book is I believe totally relevant to that modern world. I write so that it might have an impact on a society from which I have received much, but which many can see has its problems. And those problems, far from diminishing as our affluence and educational attainment rise, are it appears on the increase.

January 2005
Warrington

---

[1] Alternative Service Book 1980 (as amended in 2000)

Introduction

Society today

Our society today seems to be confused about what it means to be a man. We have seen a decline in traditional family structures where hetero-sexual marriage and male headship was the order of the day.

We see problems in our schools and rising crime rates, with a disproportionate involvement of young men. There are stresses in the traditional support structures of society in general and government agencies in particular – what is a 'partner'? Who should receive any state benefits due? Who is 'head of the household'?

I believe these things are related. The Bible shows us that one of man's key roles is to be a husband. Here he could find his place in the family and society, have an outlet for his energies and creativity, and bear the responsibility and authority for which God had uniquely suited him. It is a noble and worthy thing to be a Christian husband.

The loss of this perspective impacts strongly on many areas of life. Many of the issues that feature in newspaper and television headlines can be traced to the absence of a Christian husband in the homes of our land.

Death and disease

The sex drive is a hugely powerful life force. Without a strong moral ethic it runs through society uncontrolled and leads to broken relationships, abortions and sexually transmitted disease. At the time of writing, new infections of HIV, which causes AIDS, have risen in Britain by 20 percent since 2001, bringing the number of people living with the virus to nearly 50,000. The group most at risk in the UK continues to be gay and bisexual men, accounting in 2002 for some 80 percent (1,500) of newly diagnosed infections not acquired abroad. Cases of gonorrhoea among gay men have nearly doubled from 1,842 in 1999 to 3,363 in 2002. Syphilis infections rose from 52 to 607 during the same period.[1] In the United States, the total of those infected with HIV increases some 40,000 a year, and more than half of those were infected through male-to-male sexual contact.[2]

The problem is even greater in other areas of the world. HIV is spreading through Africa like the bubonic plague. In Sub-Saharan Africa it is estimated that more than 25 million are infected with HIV and some 2.3 million died from AIDS in 2004 alone. Life expectancy on the continent has plunged from 62 years to 45 years.[3] Estimates of future infection rates and deaths world wide are mind boggling.

Whatever the origin of the disease, most healthcare professionals admit that the spread of the disease would cease if there were no drug taking by injection, and sexual intercourse took place only between married heterosexual couples.

Divorce

The number of divorces in the UK is currently running at just over half the number of marriages contracted in recent years. The same is true for the United States.[4] Even this figure conceals the ever-growing number of people who cohabit, where a broken relationship does not figure in any statistics.

Housing

The housing shortage in the UK is not caused so much by a rising population, but by an increasing number of one-person households.[5] Similar trends can be seen in other western countries, for example in Japan[6] and the USA.[7] This is partly because people are living longer, but a big factor is the rise in divorced and separated people, and young people leaving home not to get married but to live a single life.

Single women

The feminist agenda, as predicted by Bertrand Russell, has ironically worked against women in this area. Men have been freed from the constraints of their traditional role, enabling them to have sex without responsibility or authority. They have responded in considerable numbers, like rogue elephants. They often have multiple partners, albeit serially, moving on from one to another as they become bored or the relationship becomes difficult.

This has left older single women who wish to marry having to compete with the attractions of a rising generation of younger women, many of whom seem more than willing to pander to an older man's vanity and lust.

Single parents

The one million single parents in the UK are predominantly women.[8] In the United States there are more single mothers than fathers. Statistically, one in three children are born to unmarried parents and in most cases, where separation occurs, custody of the child is awarded to the mother. It is also rare in the UK to find a man with custody of the children. It is the women who usually carry the responsibilities of childcare alone, often with the additional burden of providing financially for their children (the Child Support Agency enforcement rate on errant fathers has been low [9]).

Children

Children have also been impacted by these new trends both emotionally and financially. 76% of single UK parents in the fiscal year 2001/2002 were on Working Family Tax Credit or Income Support compared with 15% of couples with dependent children.[10] Only 1.7% of single parents had a high income compared to 17.4% of cohabiting parents and 33.5% of married parents.[11] In the United States, one child in 25 lives with neither parent, and as of 31 March 1999, 550,000 children were in foster care, a 35% increase since 1990.[12]

Children today often have many half brothers and sisters, some not knowing who their biological father is. Teacher friends have told me that in small communities this can give rise to unwitting relationships between half brothers and sisters and problems with any resultant children.

Why is this?

In the last fifty years the western world has seen a huge rise in all of these problems as it has rejected traditional Christian teaching on marriage. As a society, we have become confused about gender roles in marriage and, rejecting traditional family structures, we have found no effective substitute.

On one hand men are no longer sure what it is that women want from them. On the other hand they are more than happy to pursue a bachelor lifestyle with complete sexual expression free from the 'constraints' of marriage. Even if they do eventually marry it is later than in previous generations.[13]

In this short book I want to explore what role God had in mind for man as a husband. It is a role God created when he first brought Eve to Adam. We will consider in turn Adam's Edenic experience; God's first lessons to him; and the outworking of these things in the Old Testament. But above all, we shall find in the teaching of the New Testament what it is to be a husband – the husband that the Creator had in mind for Eve's blessing, and therefore for the benefit of all married women.

---

[1] Reuters NewMedia – Monday November 24, 2003 Reporting Dr Kevin Fenton

[2] Statistics published by AVERT, a national UK charity devoted to averting HIV worldwide (http://www.avert.org/usastatg.htm)

[3] Figures published by UNAIDS in the 'AIDS Epidemic Update 2004'.

[4] National Statistics Census 2001. Figures based on year 2000

[5] The number of people living on their own [in Britain] will soar over the next five years, transforming the consumer landscape. By 2005 Britain will have 1.7 million fewer people living as part of a family, and 1 million more people

over 50, than there were in 2000. Datamonitor report 26 November 2002

[6] See Japanese government statistics published by the Statistics Bureau on www.stat.go.jp

[7] 'Two-parent households increased 6 percent since 1990. In contrast mother headed households grew by 25 percent. Single mother households now make up 7 percent of all households. For the first time ever, less than a quarter of American households consist of nuclear families. Married couples with children now make up 24 percent of all households, compared to 39 percent in 1990. As a result of delayed marriage, an aging population, and low unemployment, there are now slightly more single-person households in the United States than there are nuclear families' An analysis of the year 2000 USA census by Council on Contemporary Families, http://www.contemporaryfamilies.org/public/families.php

[8] In a written answer to the House of Commons to a letter dated 5 April 2000 the Director of the Office for National Statistics reported that in 1999 there were an estimated 1.7 million lone parents of which 1.5 million were women. Hansard. See http://www.parliament.the-stationery-office.co.uk/pa/cm199900/cmhansrd/vo000405/text/00405w10.htm

[9] See 'Report by Comptroller and Auditor General on the Child Support Agency's Client Funds Account 2002-2003' where arrears 'considered recoverable' are recorded as £783 million – representing more than 15 months total receipts by the Agency for that year. http://www.nao.org.uk/publications/nao_reports/02-03/csa0203.pdf

[10] Figures published by the Department of Work and Pensions: http://www.statistics.gov.uk/STATBASE/Expodata/Spreadsheets/D7407.xls

[11] Office for National Statistics 11 December 2003

[12] Statistics publsihed by Women's Educational Media: http://www.womedia.org/taf_statistics.htm

[13] National Statistics Census 2001: Average age of marriage for men has gone from 27 years old to 34 years old for all bridegrooms and for single men bridegrooms from 25 years old to 30 years old over the last 30 years.

1
Some Definitions

What is a Christian?

A Christian I define, as does the Bible, to be a follower of the Lord Jesus Christ.[1] A Christian is someone who has put their whole trust in Jesus Christ, and only him, to restore their lost relationship with God.[2] The church, as defined by the Bible, consists of all those, both past and present, who love and trust in the Lord Jesus Christ.[3] A Bible-believing Christian is somebody who accepts the Bible alone as the final authority on all matters of faith and conduct.[4]

But what does all that mean – and how did I become such a Christian? I was brought up in a good family that attended church and was regularly sent to Sunday School. I ceased attending church when I was a teenager, still without any *understanding* of the great Bible truths. I cannot recall any significant biblical issue being considered at home nor did I discuss these issues with my friends. But we considered ourselves 'Christians' because we had a respectable Christian veneer.

It was only when I was a young man that I consciously heard the biblical gospel preached and was challenged to consider my own position before a holy God. Eventually I came to believe that the Lord Jesus Christ was the only way back to God – and that by changing direction in my life and believing and trusting in him I could have a new start. God enabled me to do these things and, having had my blind eyes opened by his Holy Spirit, I became a Christian and received the eternal life Christ promised. I only realised later that the faith I have in him is a faith that God himself gave me.[5] I became part of the church that has existed throughout the ages.

Over time, I came to accept that the Bible did indeed contain all I needed to know to live a life that would please my Creator and help me to lead a productive life while on earth.[4] I realised that doing what he wanted was not a case of keeping rules set by some heavenly 'park keeper', but obedience flowing from the love I had for him. In any case, what rules there were had been given for my benefit and the benefit of those around me.

It is from this biblical perspective that I attempt to outline what it is to be a Christian husband.

Marriage

Let us see if we can define different sorts of marriage.

Civil marriage is where the state recognises the coming together of a man and a woman in a sexual union that is intended to be permanent. The state then recognises for many legal and tax purposes that the two have 'become one'. So, for example, assets may pass between man and wife without taxation. The state does not lay any special duties on either partner, except where children are involved. Then either parent can be called on to provide financial support for their children if they are not so doing. The marriage can only be dissolved on certain conditions or grounds.

Religious marriage is when a couple come together with a view to a permanent sexual union and make promises to each other according to their religion. Such a marriage might or might not be registered with the state. For example, a Muslim man might take four wives, but only one wife be registered with the state, as this is all the state allows. The marriage of the non-state-registered wives can be dissolved on grounds determined by the Islamic faith. The state will not recognise more than one wife as being a legitimate partner for any state benefits.

Secular cohabitation is when two people live together in a sexual (but not necessarily hetero-sexual) relationship. The relationship is not regulated by the state or by any religion. Both are free to behave within the relationship as they see fit, or have agreed, and the relationship can be dissolved at any time. The state however may recognise a heterosexual cohabitation as being a quasi-marriage and pay benefits on that basis. For example widow's and widower's benefits may be paid by the armed services to men and women who can show they have been a long term partner of the deceased.

A cultural marriage ceremony – common in some African countries – celebrated by the couples' families and friends and recognised in the local community, but this is not a religious marriage. Nor is it recognised by the state. It is more than secular cohabitation because there is a formal public ceremony to mark the coming together of the couple. Their marriage is recognised by their community, but not by the state.

Civil partnerships. In some countries current or proposed legislation enables couples living together to register their relationship as a civil partnership and so secure some of the legal status and taxation benefits of a married couple. This is of particular interest to homosexual couples.

Anomalies have already arisen. For example, two sisters living together, or a daughter caring for her mother, might not be allowed to sign such a partnership agreement and would be disadvantaged relative to a homosexual couple. This civil partnership is a logical step for a government driven by a human rights agenda. It will clarify what is becoming a difficult area. However whenever such legislation is passed, where does it leave civil marriage – since there will be two sorts of partnership with virtually exactly the same legal and tax status?[6]

If the concept of Christian heterosexual marriage is abandoned by the state then Christians will have to make a separate decision when they marry as to whether they register the relationship as a civil partnership. There is no reason why they should not but (in those countries where it applies) the separation of the church and the state in this matter will then perhaps become more clear.

Is heterosexual cohabitation 'marriage'?

A marriage from a biblical perspective is when a man and woman come together in union having made a lifetime commitment one to the other.[7]

Union without commitment is not necessarily marriage. It is clear from the Bible that the sexual act itself does not create a marriage. If we look at the story of the Samaritan woman in John 4:15-18, we see notice that neither Jesus nor the woman saw the man she was cohabiting with as her husband. This might be helpful for some who were not sexually pure before becoming Christians – a previous relationship does not necessarily count as marriage in the eyes of God.

I hope to show that Christian marriage has little in common with the cohabitation that is so widespread today. Even a relationship formalised as marriage by a civil and legal transaction may in practice amount to little more than cohabitation.

Living together, sharing a bed, a home and certain domestic responsibilities, does not fulfil the criterion for Christian marriage. As we shall see, that criterion is that marriage should provide a picture of the relationship between Christ and the church. In such a relationship there should be total commitment of one to the other, equality of love and esteem, but distinct roles and responsibilities for the husband and the wife.

The church surrenders herself to Christ and finds fulfilment in him, and in turn he sacrificially gives himself to the church, which is then secure with him, as Jesus referring to believers as sheep emphatically says.[8]

But practically speaking?

Many Christian families (including my own) have friends and relations that are cohabiting. What should our attitude be to them? Can a long term cohabiting heterosexual couple be considered married in the eyes of God? I know this is a dilemma for many.

If it is a long term relationship in which each partner has shown commitment to the other, then perhaps the answer should be yes? As we shall see, there is no compulsion for a Christian couple to register their marriage with the state – so why should we insist on a non-Christian couple doing so? Surely what is important is the nature of the relationship and the mutual commitment.

This is a consideration that goes beyond the scope of this book, and there are strong views on either side. But it is a matter that Christian people should think about.

Christian marriage

A marriage conducted in a church building does not necessarily make a marriage a Christian marriage. Some will disagree with this statement, believing that by being held in a church the ceremony itself makes a marriage 'Christian'. After all, some believe that a baptismal service held over an infant child by an accredited minister makes the child a Christian, and it is possible to feel the same way about marriage. But this would be difficult to argue on biblical grounds. I believe a Christian marriage would be more readily described as a religious marriage that is based on biblical principles.

What confuses some is that a Christian wedding service may be accompanied by a simultaneous religious and civil marriage. In other words, there are three different things happening all at once – the personal *public* commitment of the bride and groom to each other; a marriage service approved as valid by the church; and a ceremony recognised by the state (either by virtue of the officiating minister being accredited by the state or the presence of a separate civil 'registrar').

We ought to be clear that it would be entirely possible to have a biblically valid Christian marriage without having a civil marriage. The state does not regulate individual Christians' behaviour in this area – they are governed by obedience to their Lord.

What, then, makes a Christian marriage different to cohabitation or a civil partnership?

First, a Christian marriage is heterosexual. Once you accept the reality of a creator God you have to consider not chance in the formation of creatures, but design. And design pre-supposes purpose and function. As we look at human anatomy and reproduction we see all these things – design, purpose and function. From this perspective, even without the specific teaching of the Bible, it is obvious that a man and a woman were designed to be together and to reproduce their kind. God made Eve, a woman, for Adam and brought her to him.

When we turn to the Bible we see that it is heterosexual marriage that is taught. After the specific example of Adam and Eve there is a uniform assumption in Genesis 2:24 of subsequent heterosexual unions.

There is not a single instance of a homosexual marriage in the Bible, and both the Old and New Testaments specifically condemn homosexual practices.[9]

This is not just a case of some arcane law rooted in a long gone civilisation. As we shall see in chapter 4, female and male genders were specifically created by God and are in some mysterious way a reflection of the Godhead. Later we shall see that the imagery of Christ's church in the New Testament is one of a female bride while Christ is the male bridegroom. Neither of these teachings could find their fulfilment in a homosexual union.

So a husband is a husband – not to another man but to a woman. And a woman is to be the wife of a man, not a woman. Marriage in the Bible is exclusively heterosexual. But being a hetero-sexual relationship will not necessarily make the Christian couple's marriage distinct from a heterosexual civil partnership or cohabitation.

Neither does a heterosexual couple who are sexually faithful to each other and have a marriage sanctioned by the state, necessarily have a Christian marriage – they could well be Hindus or humanists. Nor, if you accept my premise above, does having the service conducted in a church building define the true nature of the relationship.

The unique distinctives are (1) the point of reference the couple have when they make their promises to each other, and (2) how they intend to work out their roles and responsibilities – how they intend to conduct their marriage. I hope to show in this book (confining myself to the husband's role) that a couple have a Christian marriage only if they base their relationship on biblical principles and guidelines.

---

[1] Acts 11:26
[2] John 3:16
[3] 1 Corinthians 1:2
[4] 2 Timothy 3:15-17
[5] Ephesians 2:8
[6] National Statistics Census 2001 show that in 1999 only two in five

marriages in Great Britain were solemnised with a religious ceremony.

[7] Genesis 2:24

[8] John 10:28

[9] Leviticus 18:22; Romans 1:27

2
A Contemporary View of Masculinity

Vive la difference

Before we look at the biblical aspects of the husband's role it will be useful to consider the nature of masculinity and its expression today. The Bible says that God created Adam and Eve male and female – that is, he made them different from each other. He said that his design was good – very good.[1] But what were these innate differences? What is the essential nature of masculinity and femininity?

This whole subject has intrigued people since creation and at no time more than the present. Gender issues have been the subject of heated debates and many modern lawyers make a living out of legislation designed to control such issues as sexual discrimination in the workplace.

Some have sought to deny the differences, admitting only the obvious physiological and reproductive divergences.[2] But no amount of semantics or political correctness can hide what even casual observers of society can see for themselves – that men and women often think differently, have different priorities, and tend to want different things out of life. And it is not just to casual observers – differences between the sexes have emerged in all sorts of behavioural research over the years. These differences, it seems, are not always determined by culture and environment, but emerge even during the first days of life.[3]

If there are no fundamental gender differences, why does the publishing industry market so many magazines and periodicals as written 'for women'? Even BBC Radio 4 persists with 'Woman's Hour'. A considerable amount of time is spent in Western consumer society establishing our identity as males or females. Marketing executives in the car, fashion or music industries would ignore gender-specific consumer spending at their peril.

So it seems that men differ from women in many ways other than physical; but what exactly are these differences? Male and female characteristics occupy a spectrum, and no single trait is a definitive marker of masculinity or femininity. While some traits are more indicative of gender than others, it is still difficult to define masculinity or femininity, and even less so today than 50 years ago.

To be a man

Despite the modern tendency to blur roles, the adolescent male is still keen to pursue his 'maleness' – to establish his manhood. He wants to find out who he is – as a person and as a man. He likes to belong to a specifically masculine cohort, to wear the right trainers, support the right football team, to use the right expressions, and go to the 'in' places. But there is no rule book that says definitively what it is to be a man.

I think for a woman it has traditionally been easier. She is uniquely equipped by nature to give birth and nurture new life. But having fathered a child, a man has no biological indicators of what to do next. His role in child-rearing is not determined biologically, but largely by the customs of the society in which he lives. Today, as the young man looks out on his contemporary world, he sees a mass of confusion about what exactly that role is.

A tricky question

If you are not convinced that confusion exists, ask a respected friend or colleague (male or female) to define masculinity. If they struggle to do so, think how much more the average adolescent male might have difficulty defining his role, let alone fulfilling it.

John Dunbar, an American soldier, was played by Kevin Costner in the film 'Dances with Wolves'. As Dunbar integrates more and more into his adopted Sioux Indian tribe, he begins to realise his true worth.

This comes home to him after a closely fought battle against a rival tribe. They were fighting to protect their women and children and food store that were, as Dunbar comments, 'only feet from them'.

He was not fighting in some distant land for an unclear cause. He had found a clear role to play – the Sioux warrior man.

Tribal cultures often have clear-cut roles for their men, into which adolescents are initiated by some ceremony. Having achieved 'manhood' they are then expected to play a defined, manly and respected role according to the cultural traditions of his tribe.

But the modern, urban-dwelling males of Western civilisation have long ago abandoned the gender-specific roles of 'primitive' tribes. Instead we have specialisation – soldiers fight wars, policemen maintain order, politicians make laws, butchers provide meat and bakers bread.

Until the last 20 or 30 years or so, to have chosen a 'masculine' job might have defined your masculinity. But now – and rightly so – women are achieving similar status in similar jobs, and fewer and fewer careers are considered a masculine preserve. In today's Western culture a young man is left largely without any obvious means to establish his masculinity – except negative ones.

Macho man

Some seek escape from this dilemma in negative ways – by doing things that women tend not to do. Male-specific antisocial behaviour offer them (they believe) a way to stake their claim in the masculine world – often through imitation of their peers.

It is a fact that women rarely commit acts of vandalism or indeed any violent crime. The young male, by contrast, finds easy entry to a male sub-culture defined by anti-social behaviour patterns. This is an attractive option for some, especially those who find it difficult to get regular or satisfying employment. Male unemployment rates nationally are more than double female unemployment rates.[4]

In the possibly subconscious view of many youths today, certain sorts of anti-social behaviour mark him as a 'man' and simultaneously feed his masculine need for risk-taking. All too often it also wins the recognition of his peer group. This expression of masculinity fills our courts and prisons – certainly the prison population in UK is rising inexorably at the present time. Governments of different persuasions try to reduce the number of custodial sentences being handed out by the courts, but despite ever increasing spending on education, social services and the probation services, the crime rate continues to rise. It is a phenomenon that seems common to most affluent western democracies.

Vulnerable man

So, unlike John Dunbar who fought for a clear and just cause as a Sioux warrior, our young man's desire for adventure, and his need to be recognised as a man, has failed to find a positive outlet. Some believe this inability to find a satisfying role is contributing to the rising incidence of mental health problems among young men. The most common cause of death for males until their late twenties is now suicide.[5]

For seven years, until March 2000, I was chairman of a health authority, and during that time the board of directors sanctioned more than a billion pounds worth of health care expenditure. Equality was one of our priorities, but we made no impact on the differential between the male and female death rates – the male death rate always being higher.

Our partner agencies always showed the preponderance of men in their reported statistics, whether in unemployment rates, imprisonment, drug taking, accidents, or suicide. At present I am chairman of a homeless charity that caters not just for homeless people but those that are considered vulnerable. Male service users out number females by three to one. Logic would determine that there should be a government minister for men, rather than women!

For a society to praise and encourage feminine traits while portraying perceived masculine traits as negative – to try and sublimate the latter and offer no positive outlet – is a recipe for male discontent. There is a danger that young men move into adulthood feeling alienated in a feminised culture in which they find it difficult to participate. They can retreat into a laddish sub culture – a single man's world free from family responsibilities where they are able to indulge the baser expressions of their masculinity.

And what is the effect on a new generation of young women of this 'identity crisis' that afflicts so many young men? They find themselves in the Bridget Jones generation, complaining that there are no suitable men for them as life partners. They should be alert to this trend and consider what it is that they want from men.

A biblical role?

Perhaps it is impossible to agree what masculinity is. But we know that God made the first man, so he must have had a role in mind for him! So rather than trying to define masculinity by looking for particular 'masculine' traits, would it not be better to see if we can discover what that distinctive role might be? Then men could work out their masculinity, and find their fulfilment in that role.

Instead of accepting the status quo and the received wisdom of our age, I believe we should look again at the Bible. If we do we shall find that it does indeed offer a distinctive role for males. Men in turn should – in the light of the Bible's timeless teaching – re-evaluate what it is to be a man. They should seek to know how their masculinity can be constructively expressed in the social structures God has defined for his creation – namely, the church, the state, but particularly the family.

I hope to show that it is in the family that the man has his most distinctive role – that of a Christian husband. But first let us go back to the beginning.

---

[1] Genesis 1:31

[2] See Acknowledgements in "The Essential Difference" by Professor Simon Baron-Cohen. Professor Cohen states that to publish his book he considered 'risky' in these 'politically dangerous waters' and so delayed publication for several years.

[3] Research by Connellan & Batkti quoted on page 57 "The Essential Difference" by Professor Simon Baron-Cohen Penguin 2003.

[4] Cheshire County Council Research and Intelligence Unit September 2003

[5] National UK Census 2001: 'There has been a marked increase in suicide death rates in people aged 15 to 24 since the end of the 1950s. Between 1971 and 1997 the suicide death rate for men aged 15 to 24 rose from 6.9 per

100,000 population in to 16.4 per 100,000 population. For women in this age group there was a fall from the mid-1970s to the mid-1980s, and the rate was 4.0 per 100,000 population in 1997. Suicide among men aged 25 to 44 has risen since the 1950s to a level higher than among any other group. Rates among those over the age of 44 have declined. Suicide rates are associated with mental health problems, such as depression.'

3
In the Beginning

A perfect world

Before time began God decided to create a physical universe for himself – and in that universe he placed our wonderful world. This world was made so perfect that if we saw it today it would take our breath away. We read about it in the opening chapters of the Bible.

More than any previous generation we have been allowed a glimpse of that lost world. Computer graphics used in recent television programmes have brought to life what previously we knew only in two dimensions. We see pictures of huge majestic beasts striding across landscapes rich with amazing flowers and plants drenched in the warmth of tropical sunshine. The programme makers are no friends of the Bible, of course, but they unwittingly provide us with a glimpse of God's original perfect creation.

At the pinnacle of this creation was a man – God called him Adam. Some say he might have been tall and handsome[1] but all we know for certain is that Adam's genes contained all the potential of the human race. Certainly, God said of all his creation that it was 'very good' and Adam was not short of brain power, having the ability to name all the animals God brought before him.

Despite his glorious home in 'the garden of Eden', Adam was not completely fulfilled. So God caused Adam to go into a deep sleep and formed the first woman, Eve, from his side. God brought Eve to Adam and at last Adam saw what he wanted – not a beast of the field but a true companion – 'bone of my bones and flesh of my flesh' (Gen. 3:23).

Eve was created to be a 'helper' to Adam (Gen. 2:20). Lest we are distracted by that word and its modern connotation of inferiority, we need to remember that in the Old Testament God himself is described as a 'helper' – the helper of Israel,[2] the helper of the fatherless,[3] and the helper of David.[4]

It was all God's idea

So humans were created 'male and female'. This was God's idea, his specific intent. Furthermore, the Bible says that 'in the image of God he created him; male and female he created them' (Gen. 1:27). So Eve was not just a companion to Adam. In some mysterious way, Adam and Eve together are a reflection of God himself.

Our human sexuality, then, has its origins in the nature of the Godhead. Our maleness and femaleness is not an aberration – a function of reproduction, a 'spin' on our true selves imposed by our culture. Rather, it reflects the nature of God as a moral and rational Being and is designed to fulfil God's purposes in the world he has created. It is from this exalted perspective that a Christian must approach the subject of gender roles.

Another story

I know that macro-evolutionary theory tells a different story. It proposes that out of some primeval chemical 'soup' (the origin of which no theory can tell us) appeared the first living organism (by processes unknown). Through successive generations, this organism accumulated chance mutations, which were 'selected' by the environment to produce a higher life-form. The millennia passed and these creatures 'gave birth' to other more sophisticated life forms. Millions of years (and countless deaths) later, the first man emerged from ape-hood.

But the Bible denies that the first man walked on the corpses of a billion pre-Adamic creatures.[5] He was created 'right first time'. He was not the product of a million cul-de sacs of a blind process that, quite by chance, threw up a thinking being equipped with self-consciousness and a conscience. Adam was made by a loving God who breathed life into him to make him a living being (Gen. 2:7). The contrast could hardly be greater. The implications of these divergent creation accounts profoundly affect our world-view – the way we perceive the creation, our purpose in it, and (more specifically for this book) our gender roles.

A divine role

Eve was to support Adam in his divine commission. Together they were told what their task was: 'God blessed them and said to them, "Be fruitful and increase in number; fill the earth and subdue it. Rule over the fish of the sea and the birds of the air and over every living creature that moves on the ground"' (Gen. 1:28).

Everything was set for an idyllic life in an earthly paradise. So what went wrong?

Adam and Eve it seems were on probation. There was something they must not do – as recorded in Genesis 2:16-17, 'And the LORD God commanded the man, "You are free to eat from any tree in the garden; but you must not eat from the tree of the knowledge of good and evil, for when you eat of it you will surely die."'

A wrong turn

You could almost write the script even if you did not know the Bible. Yes, Adam and Eve ate from that tree. A creature in the garden (a fallen angel as we learn later) talked Eve into thinking it was a good idea after all – even though she told him correctly that it was precisely what God had forbidden. Adam obviously went along with this, happy to eat what his wife offered him.

Speculations about the significance of the tree, or why Adam and Eve had to be on probation, or what this creature was doing in Eden in the first place, have filled many books and exercised many minds in the millennia since. Suffice it to say that the consequences for Adam and Eve, and for our world as a whole, were disastrous. God had promised death – and God 'is not a man that he should lie' (Num. 23:19). Death is what happened.

It was a 'spiritual' death. Our first couple lost contact with God, no longer happy to walk and talk with their creator. In fact, they hid – first from each other when they made coverings for themselves, and then from God. Later – much later in our human time frame – came their physical death. Adam and Eve returned to the earth from which they came.

Death from Adam

We notice here another contrast with current humanistic thought. Evolution teaches that Adam came from death – from countless generations of precursors. The Bible teaches that death came from Adam.

And what a death it was! It carried not only Adam and Eve to their graves but their contemporary living world with them. Nature became red in tooth and claw. The whole creation, says Paul, became subject to corruption and futility (Rom. 8:20-21).

And – importantly for us - Adam took us with him. The Bible teaches that we were all 'in Adam' when he sinned. We were in his loins waiting to be born. What he did we did. He was our representative. So when he lost his relationship with God we all did – we are all born spiritually dead, not knowing God. We are born into the same spiritual and physical condition in which Adam and Eve now found themselves – mortal and unaware of God (Rom. 3:9-12).

This is one of the reasons why there is so much religious confusion in our world – God is 'hidden' from us. Because of this many come to the remarkable conclusion (rather like a young child playing hide and seek) that because we cannot see him, he cannot see us – or even is not there at all.

All humanity thus shares Adam's two-fold death. We are born out of communion with God and we all die physically. Of all the uncertainties in life, death is not one of them. Grimly, we all involved in what theologians call 'the Fall'.

This all might seem very unfair, but Adam was our 'federal head'. We are familiar with the concept but in another context. The federal head of the USA is, at the time of writing, their president, George W.

Bush. What he says for America goes. So when he declared war on Iraq in 2003, all USA was at war with Iraq, even though most individual Americans played no part in that decision.

Why God chose to deal with us in this federal way we do not know. But who could honestly claim that if they had not fallen with Adam they would themselves have lived a sinless life? The fact that God is prepared to deal with humanity in this federal way turned out to our great advantage.

Because all was not lost for Adam and Eve. God promised a way back. In the distant future as it turned out, he was going to provide a Saviour, who would be the woman's 'seed'. That saviour is the Lord Jesus Christ – the 'second Adam' and federal head of all who believe. As we lost everything in Adam, men and women were to be restored in Christ. Those who have Christ as their representative in heaven are restored to spiritual communion with God and one day will walk with God forever in a new and greater 'Eden' called heaven.

Life goes on

But what of Adam and Eve after that terrible day? As is so often the case, God's justice was tempered by his mercy. Their marriage wasn't over. Rather, It became God's institution, to be available for all mankind and all time. He intended it to continue even in the fallen world.

Adam and Eve had to work out with God's help what it was he wanted of them and what they should expect from each other in the new situation they faced. They duly continued together as a married couple, had children and eventually died.

The family became God's basic unit for human society. He created that first family and from these early chapters of Genesis we can learn much about ourselves and the role God has for gender in the family and in society generally.

The rest of the Old Testament slowly unfolds God's redemption plan, as he works through individuals and then through the nation of Israel. From these Scriptures we see how God directs individual men and women and how teaches them about himself.

Our true identity

It is only in the context of creation that I believe we can find our true identity, and when we have found this find our intended role in life.

We need to know our origins, to go back to our beginning. It is when a man (or a woman, but for our purposes we are talking about men) comes to realise that he has a creator God and seeks him out, that he is making the first steps on a journey to find himself – and thus for a man find his true manhood.

If on this journey he turns to the New Testament he will soon see that the only way to find the one true God is in Jesus Christ. We learn that God has provided a way back to himself, and that way is for us to believe in the Saviour he has provided.

We are to accept that he alone made a sufficient sacrifice to pay the price for that first disobedience in Eden. And that only by coming to faith in Jesus Christ and accepting his claim on our lives will we find a way back into Eden. Here once again we can have fellowship with God and resume our earthly task with his approval.

And more than that, the Eden that Jesus Christ eventually brings us to is not just an earthly paradise – but a heavenly one. He fulfilled the probationary conditions that Adam and Eve failed with and Jesus has promised to take those that believe to a place where there will be no tears, no pain, and no death.

But we are moving on too quickly, so lets look at what God said to Adam specifically and see what we can learn from that first couple about role relationships in marriage.

Adam as the first husband

The Bible tells of an amazing, wonderful, loving, but above all holy God who is ultimately beyond the grasp of our intellect or imagination. When it turns its spotlight on the human story it equally tells us as it is – it does not hide our human frailty and failings.

We need to bear this in mind as we consider the men that God chose to work through at the beginning of history, the first man Adam and the subsequent key people in the Bible story – Noah, Abraham, Isaac, Jacob and others. These are the father's of our faith – the 'patriarchs'.

The men here revealed and their various activities do not all provide good examples of manhood nor do they all make ideal husbands. But despite, and even because of this, we can hopefully learn from them and see by the way God deals with them what it was God had in mind for the role of men in general and husbands in particular.

As we have seen, God had created Adam first. And then he decided 'it is not good for the man to be alone. I will make a helper suitable for him' (Gen. 2:18); so Eve was created. She was created from Adam and brought to him. What a meeting that must have been. They were given to each other for their mutual benefit, Eve to Adam, Adam to Eve.

They had virtually complete freedom in their garden idyll. As we have seen there was just one thing they were not to do, but it was just the one thing that they had done. It was from this event that all our troubles began. God punished them by breaking the relationship He had with them and allowing death and disease to come into their perfect world.

Having spoke to Eve and then the serpent, God as the divine judge, having listened to the evidence, turned to Adam, the defendant, and began to pronounce his judgement.

God explained the consequences for him and for all mankind and outlined the future course of history (Gen. 3:17-19):

> To Adam he said, "Because you listened to your wife and ate from the tree about which I commanded you, 'You must not eat of it,' "Cursed is the ground because of you; through painful toil you will eat of it all the days of your life. It will produce thorns and thistles for you, and you will eat the plants of the field. By the sweat of your brow you will eat your food until you return to the ground, since from it you were taken; for dust you are and to dust you will return."

'Because you have listened to your wife'. Did the Lord not intend Adam to listen to his wife – the woman he had given to him for companionship? Surely yes. So where had Adam gone wrong? To find this out we need to see if we can deduce what God expected of Adam.

Adam - a leadership role

Theologians who know about these things often say there is significance in that Adam was created before Eve and therefore was 'senior' to her. Certainly cultures in biblical times took this view, in that the first born was of especial significance to the family and had a greater share in any inheritance. Even in our own contemporary Britain the eldest child (often even into old age) is seen to be the most senior and the one expected to take additional responsibility. These same theologians think there is significance in that Adam named Eve implying some sort of pre-eminence or authority for Adam.

Whatever our view of these things, I think we can see from the story itself that right at the beginning it does seem that God expected Adam to take some lead in the garden paradise. It was specifically to Adam that God gave the instructions as to what could and could not be done there (Gen. 2:17).

It was specifically of Adam that he asked 'Where are you?', when they *both* had hidden after their disobedience.

Adam answered and the subsequent initial exchange is with Adam (Gen. 3:8-12). God only speaks to Eve when Adam blames her for their predicament: 'The man said, "The woman you put here with me–she gave me some fruit from the tree, and I ate it"' (Gen. 3:12).

So it seems clear that before the Fall God was looking to Adam to exercise some leadership in their joint rule of his creation. But Adam was quick to abdicate any leadership role he had in the marriage. Instead of insisting with Eve that what she suggested was wrong, he went along with her proposal. When he was 'found out' he proceeded to blame God for having given him the woman in the first place. He refused to take any responsibility for his actions.

What had gone wrong? It is not difficult to see. Adam had failed to obey God. He had 'listened to his wife' when he knew better. It is not that he had not told her of God's specific command – she knew it well enough. That was not Adam's failure. He had failed to impress on Eve the importance of that original instruction given to him by God, he had not taken the lead, he had let Eve take the wrong step.

Things changed

Whatever the situation was before their disobedience the Bible is clear that after this Adam was to have rule over Eve: 'To the woman he said, "I will greatly increase your pains in childbearing; with pain you will give birth to children. Your desire will be for your husband, and he will rule over you"' (Gen. 3:16).

There are nuances to the interpretation of this verse, in that perhaps Eve was going to be subject to Adam because of her attraction to him. In other words, her need of male companionship meant that she would be was always looking to please a man. It is perhaps possible to see an outworking of this in the huge expenditure that women make in our culture on clothes, make up and even cosmetic surgery.

It is a sad fact in our fallen world that the word 'rule' often has a negative ring to it. But we must distinguish between God's intentions and instructions to us and its application by fallen men and women in our history and contemporary society. We will deal with the application of a husband's 'rule' more fully in chapter 10.

Some consider that Adam's rule was a direct consequence of the fall alone and like other consequences, pain and disease for example, we should do our best to ameliorate their effects.

It is certainly the case that women have suffered at the hands of men as a consequence of the entrance of sin into the world, and the whole matter of sexual relationships and childbirth were complicated by it – as was every area of life.

Perhaps God was saying here that man's rule would be now more obvious and onerous for the woman. God's original plan included procreation by Adam and Eve (Gen. 1:28). Only now in a fallen world procreation was not only necessary to populate the world, but to replace each dying generation. It could be that a woman's original menstrual cycle was just once a year, or even every decade? But now women would be more vulnerable having to give birth far more often than would have been necessary in a pre-fall world.

If Genesis chapter 3 stood alone we might well take this as the entire explanation. But as we have seen the situation before the fall appears to suggest different roles for Adam and Eve, and as the rest of the

Bible story unfolds there is no attempt to reverse these roles. Indeed as we shall see later the very roles themselves are a reflection of redemption's story in Christ and the church.

Certainly the consequences of the Fall soon unravel. Adam and Eve have their first child Cain, and then later Able was born. Cain committed the first murder killing his own brother. Cain went on to have a son Enoch. Five generations after this Lamech was born, he had two wives[6] and they both had to endure his ugly boast in Genesis 4:23-24:

> Lamech said to his wives, "Adah and Zillah, listen to me; wives of Lamech, hear my words.I have killed a man for wounding me, a young man for injuring me. If Cain is avenged seven times, then Lamech seventy-seven times."

We can see already that we are far from that Edenic paradise.

---

[1] A view taken by Dr Kent Hovind of Creation Science Evangelism of Florida USA

[2] Deuteronomy 33:29

[3] Psalm 10:14

[4] Psalm 27:9

[5] Romans 5:12

[6] To have more than one wife does not appear to have been God's intention as we read Genesis but many Old Testament believers adopted this practice. It has been disapproved of by the christian church throughout its history.

4
An Old Testament Perspective

We now briefly scan God's dealings with men and women in the era between Adam and Eve's fall from grace and the birth of our Lord Jesus Christ. In other words, we want to get a perspective from the Old Testament on the issue of gender and role-responsibilities in a fallen world before the coming of Christ.

Men only?

But first a note about patriarchal societies (ones in which men predominantly occupy positions of authority). Some take the view that such societies are intrinsically defective because they have sometimes led to the subjugation of women. But many things are abused in any society – including money, sex, and economic power – without necessarily invalidating the model on which that society is constructed.

The fact is that the Old Testament portrays an unashamedly patriarchal society which was of God's own making. Nowhere is the impression given that God was just accepting the status quo so as not to upset contemporary feelings – making the most of a societal structure that was simply outside his control.

It seems to me that a patriarchal society existed in those early days because God *wanted it that way*, and not because such a culture emerged as a consequence of the fall whether he liked it or not.

He ordained things to be the way they were. He spoke through men. Instructions were given to *men* about what he expected and how he was to be worshiped. The great promises about the future were also given to men. He held the men accountable to him.

Noah

But let us get back to the story. A descendant of Adam and Eve's third son Seth – Noah we are told – found favour in the eyes of God (Gen. 6:8). He was a family man, married with three sons. Noah believed God and did what God told him. God had decided to destroy the world he had made with a flood – Noah's family alone was to be saved.

Noah built his famous ark precisely as God told him, to protect his wife, his sons and their wives. God gave this task to Noah – it was *his* job, not his wife's responsibility. So, at this turning point in human history, we find God talking to the man Noah as the head and representative of his family – making it clear to him that he was responsible for them.

The cataclysmic flood came, but Noah had done his job well. His family found safety in the ark. More than a year later, they emerged from the ark into a new world. Most of the old world (what modern historians would probably call the pre-historic world) had been wiped out by the catastrophic flood.

God made a new covenant with Noah.[1] Here again, Noah was the representative of his family – indeed, of the whole human race.

Abraham

Noah and his family (and thus mankind) had been given a new beginning. Eventually a descendant of Shem (Noah's first son) was born called Abram – to be renamed Abraham. God spoke to Abraham and promised to make of him a great nation.[2]

Despite God's favour towards him, Abraham fails dismally as a husband when, during their stay in Egypt and out of fear for his life, he passes his wife off as his sister. Pharaoh takes Sarah as *his* wife and Abraham enjoys the spoils of his deceit as the Egyptian ruler enriches Abraham in gratitude for his 'sister'.[3] Even the unbelieving Pharaoh was shocked when he discovered the truth – and sent Abraham and Sarah packing.[4]

Clearly, to be an ideal husband is not just a case of imitating the 'heroes of faith' and following their example! We have to discern the purpose of God in the outworking of this narrative – to understand what he would have wanted.

It is not difficult to see that Abraham was wrong in allowing Sarah to be taken by another man. He should have stood his ground and told the truth to Pharaoh to protect his wife's honour, even at the risk of his own life. God had to intervene directly to rectify the situation.[5]

Nevertheless, God – ever gracious – repeats his promises to a still childless and doubting couple, saying specifically that Abraham would have a son of his own.

Not content with this – and in a scenario strangely reminiscent of our initial fall – Sarah comes up with a plan to give God a helping hand! Abraham goes along with the idea of conceiving the promised child by Sarah's maidservant Hagar. Sarah was wrong, of course. But the responsibility for this sinful debacle surely lay with Abraham. God had given an unambiguous promise to him, and he should have said no to Sarah.

Again, as with Adam, we see the consequences of weak leadership – far from being the child of promise, Hagar's son Ishmael was to be a child of sorrow. God said: 'He will be a wild donkey of a man; his hand will be against everyone and everyone's hand against him, and he will live in hostility toward all his brothers' (Gen. 16:2).

Isaac

Eventually Sarah did give birth – to Isaac. At the age of forty, Isaac married Rebekah and loved her.[6] Isaac prayed to God on behalf of his wife because she was barren, and the twins Jacob and Esau were born.[7] Isaac favoured Esau and Rebekah favoured Jacob.[8]

Thus Isaac took the lead in their prayer life but failed to exercise wise family leadership. He not only allowed favouritism in the family but was party to it himself. Also, rather surprisingly, he made the identical mistake as his father Abraham, in trying to pass his wife off as his sister to protect his own life.[9]

Jacob

The story continues with Jacob, who falls in love with Rachel.[10] Tricked by his uncle Laban he ends up marrying both Laban's daughters – Rachel and Leah.

Upset that she is not bearing children, Rachel talks Jacob into having children with her maidservant. So history repeats itself. The whole sorry tale is told in Genesis 30 and does not read well for Jacob. Pulled this way and that by his two wives, he was unable or unwilling to take the lead.

Nevertheless, it is with Jacob that God meets.[11] It is to Jacob as head of his family that God speaks. Jacob was renamed Israel and his sons became the heads of the twelve tribes that eventually formed the great nation Israel.

A chosen nation

Space forbids us looking at all the men who feature in the Patriarchal period, but even a casual reading of this portion of Scripture reveals that leadership, authority, and responsibility – for the nation, the priesthood and the home – rested chiefly with men.

God delivered his people from enslavement in Egypt, raising up Moses as their leader. Through his mediation the nation received the ten commandments and many other laws. The Levitical priesthood was set up – for Adam had lost communion with God in Eden and the people needed priests to represent them before God. The priests were always to be men (but there was no prohibition on their marrying!)

And it was a man – Joshua – whom God raised up to lead the nation into the promised land.

Judges

After entering this land of promise, the nation was for a time ruled by Judges. God raised up these men to lead the Israelites against their enemies. And they were all men, with one remarkable exception – Deborah.

In fact this really is the exception that proves the rule. Deborah demonstrates that God could work through a woman in a position of authority if he chose to do so. It was not an impossibility for God to use a woman in this way. There was no secret taboo that prevented women being put into positions of responsibility.

Judges 4, verse 4, tells us: 'Deborah, a prophetess, the wife of Lappidoth, was leading Israel at that time.' By all accounts she was a strong and vigorous ruler – perhaps the Margaret Thatcher of her day!

But the very fact that God could choose to work through *anyone*, male or female, makes it all the more significant that he nearly always chose men when it came to the exercise of responsibility, authority and leadership.

Kings and prophets

The Old Testament relates how Israel tired of being led by Judges and demanded a king like the surrounding nations. So God consented and the kingdom was inaugurated. But there is no record of a queen ruling over Israel. Undoubtedly king's wives exercised varying degrees of influence over their husbands, but when recorded in Scripture this was usually harmful rather than helpful. Again, it was God's choice to have men in these main positions of responsibility, though godly women like Ruth and Ester were also given influential roles in God's unfolding purpose.

Finally, of course, the prophets whom God sent continually to teach and warn his people, and whose prophecies were recorded as Old Testament Scripture, were all men.

Lessons for us

What lessons can we learn from all this? The first lesson must be about God's grace, or unmerited favour. These leaders, though raised up and appointed by God, were nearly all flawed characters. From Adam in his primal disobedience, through Jacob conniving with Rachel to have children by her maidservant, to dysfunctional judges and errant kings – even the great King David was involved in adultery and murder – we see a catalogue of human sin and failure. Yet, while not condoning or ignoring their many weaknesses, God chose to speak directly to them and work out his purposes through them.

Secondly, as rulers or prophets among his people, God expected these men to exercise the leadership entrusted to them.

Thirdly, though we know little about the private family lives of these men, we know that most had wives and children for which they considered themselves responsible. Certainly the patriarchs took responsibility for the protection and shelter of their families (for example Noah and the Ark, Jacob and his family) and for family worship.[12]

In conclusion, then, male leadership was the order of the day throughout the Old Testament – whether at our origins; in our fall from that first idyllic state; during and after the destruction of the world by flood; or in leading the nation through which God chose to work. These men demonstrated every human frailty, but God persisted with the principle that men should take the lead – in the nation, in the worship of God, and in their responsibility for their families.

The following chapters will consider which, if any, of these lessons we can carry over into the Christian era and apply to our concept of a Christian husband.

---

[1] Genesis 9:1-17
[2] Genesis 12:1-3
[3] Genesis 12:10-16
[4] Genesis 12:17-20
[5] Genesis 12:17
[6] Genesis 24:67
[7] Genesis 25:21-26
[8] Genesis 27:28
[9] Genesis 26:7-11
[10] Genesis 29:18
[11] Genesis 32:22-32
[12] Genesis 31:53-55

5
Jesus Christ, the Man

A Saviour was promised many times in the Old Testament, and in Isaiah we are told he is to be 'a son'. Isaiah 9:6: 'For to us a child is born, to us a son is given, and the government will be on his shoulders. And he will be called Wonderful Counselor, Mighty God, Everlasting Father, Prince of Peace.'

We are so used to thinking of Jesus as our Saviour that we perhaps forget to consider his masculinity. This masculinity was not incidental – God had promised a boy. And eventually that boy was born, conceived of the Holy Spirit in the Virgin Mary.[1]

He grew into manhood in a humble Galilean home, preparing for the three years of earthly ministry that culminated with his pre-ordained death on the cross.

Jesus Christ was the perfect man – 'tempted in all points as we are yet without sin' (Heb. 4:12). So how did he conduct himself as a man? And is there anything we can learn from the New Testament narratives concerning his life on earth that we can apply to the role of a husband?

A man who loved much

Jesus shows himself repeatedly as a compassionate man. Right at the beginning of his ministry Jesus and his mother are at a wedding in Cana and the host runs out of wine. Even though Jesus tells his mother that it is not yet time to reveal his true identity, he accedes to her request

– turning water into wine and sparing the host of the wedding from embarrassment.[2]

Jesus also showed great wisdom and tact in dealing with his fellow man. He deals with people according to his knowledge of them. He refused to be drawn by the Pharisees, 'for he knew what was in a man' (John 2:24-25). We see him next in John's gospel interact with Nicodemus, getting straight to the point with this great teacher of the law. Yet later with the Samaritan woman (John 4) he works round to his point more gently, drawing the woman into an all-important conversation about her position before God. He *knew* men and women and sought to meet their need on the basis of that knowledge.

The 'rich young ruler' came to Jesus asking the most important question of all – 'what must I do to inherit eternal life?' Jesus rehearsed the last six commandments and the young man claimed somewhat remarkably that he had kept them all.

Although this could only have been true in terms of outward observance, we are nevertheless told that Jesus 'looked at him and loved him' (Mark 10:21). This man eventually went away with sorrow because he had not heard what he wanted to hear - yet he was loved by Christ.

The disciple John was so amazed that Jesus could love him that he often referred to himself as the 'disciple whom Jesus loved.'[3] In several places Jesus talks specifically of his love for his disciples.[4]

Lazarus, Mary and Martha were brother and sisters well known to Jesus. In John chapter 11 we read that 'Jesus loved Martha and her sister and Lazarus' (John 11:5). The sisters sent word to Jesus to tell him 'Lord the one you *love* is sick' (John 11:3). When Jesus arrived at the tomb of his friend Lazarus we are told he wept, and the Jews present said 'See how he loved him!' (John 11:34-36).

The miracles Jesus did in his earthly ministry were signs that he was the expected Messiah.[5] But if we look at the miracles themselves they were always done out of compassion for his fellow man, never just as signs to display his power. In fact he refused to be drawn into doing that.[6] Instead he healed people, fed them, and even raised some from the dead, out of compassion and love for humanity.

And of course Jesus loved his Father: 'But the world must learn that I love the Father and that I do exactly what my Father has commanded me' (John 14:31).

What greater love than Calvary?

But what greater love can anybody show for his fellow man than that he is prepared to lay down his life for them? John tells us: 'It was just before the Passover Feast. Jesus knew that the time had come for him to leave this world and go to the Father. Having loved his own who were in the world, he now showed them the full extent of his love' (John 13:1).

Calvary was surely the greatest outpouring of love the world has ever seen. Truly, love to the unlovely was shown in this, the world's most selfless act.

Jesus was a man who loved much. His was not a fickle, sentimental love, but a love born out of compassion and according to knowledge. It was a love that resulted in action – courageous and dramatic action toward the object of his love, the church.

A man who took responsibility

Supremely, Jesus took the responsibility for the great mission given him by the Father, that of securing the church. So he left his heavenly home, came to our world and offered himself as a sacrifice for sin, so that we could be forgiven and restored. Though he was rich (in heaven), Jesus became poor for our sakes, assuming the form of a servant.[7]

And he did not disappoint. He fulfilled the task the Father gave him. Jesus could pray to his Father: 'I have finished the work which you have given me to do ... While I was with them, I protected them and kept them safe by that name you gave me. None has been lost except the one doomed to destruction so that Scripture would be fulfilled' (John 17:4, 12).

He took responsibility for his great work even when he shrank from doing it. He cried out to his Father in Gethsemane while he awaited his arrest: 'My Father, if it is possible, may this cup be taken from me. But not as I will, but as you will' (Matthew 26:39).

Jesus also took responsibility in many lesser situations in the New Testament. He fed the crowds that followed him.[8] And when he could no longer take responsibility for his mother as he was dying on the cross, John 19:26-27 records that '....he turned to the disciple he loved and said [to Mary], "Dear woman here is your son" and to the disciple

"Here is your mother". From that time on the disciple took her into his home.'

Jesus accepted great responsibilities and faithfully discharged them – first as a man but supremely as our Saviour, paying the ultimate price in his voluntary separation from his Father and in his death on the cross.

A man of authority

Let us remind ourselves who this man Christ Jesus is. Colossians 1:15-17 says:

> He is the image of the invisible God, the firstborn over all creation. For by him all things were created: things in heaven and on earth, visible and invisible, whether thrones or powers or rulers or authorities; all things were created by him and for him. He is before all things, and in him all things hold together. And he is the head of the body, the church; he is the beginning and the firstborn from among the dead, so that in everything he might have the supremacy.

So it should come as no surprise that as a man he demonstrated great authority and courage in his earthly ministry. We read that: 'When Jesus had finished saying these things, the crowds were amazed at his teaching, because he taught as one who had authority, and not as their teachers of the law' (Matthew 27:28, 29).

He said of himself that 'All authority in heaven and on earth has been given to me' (Matthew 28:18).

When Jesus went up to the temple he was dismayed to see the money changers and cattle traders dominating the Gentile court. He made a whip of cords and drove out the animals and money changers and turned over their tables.[9]

Jesus was also a leader of men. With authority he calls his disciples – ordinary working men who leave everything to be with him as they respond to the master's call.[10]

He was not afraid of difficult questions and did not dissemble when confrontation was unavoidable. He answered the catch-question about paying taxes to the occupying Roman powers with his famous words,

'Give to Caesar what is Caesar's, and to God what is God's' (Matthew 22:21).

When necessary he confronted the powerful Pharisees – even telling them at one point 'you [belong to] your father the devil" (John 8:44).

Yet Jesus did not stand on his obvious authority. He rarely made a show of it. So his first appearance in the New Testament as a grown man is at the Jordan, being baptised by John the Baptist. Even though as the Son of God he was greater than his cousin John, he was happy to submit to John's baptism – to 'fulfill all righteousness' (Matthew 3:13-17).

And how did the Father respond to this? 'This is my Son, whom I love; with him I am well pleased' (Matthew 3:17).

Our heavenly father was pleased with Christ's humility and submission. Jesus Christ had unsurpassed authority and yet amazing humility. Those two things really can go together.

Although Jesus could be humble he never denied what he was. In John 8:52-54, while affirming that he is greater than Abraham he says that the honour he has comes from God. He spoke truthfully and clearly answering specific questions about himself.

A faithful man

Jesus was a loyal and faithful friend to many – Lazarus, Mary, and Martha, for example – but particularly to the disciples. How many times they misunderstood him and let him down, not least in Gethsemane when they could not even stay awake to support him in his great trial. Yet he comforts them and prays for them (John 14:1-3; 17:6-19).

But above all he was faithful to his heavenly Father in that he finished the task he was sent to do, regardless of the personal cost to himself.[11]

A perfect man

Jesus Christ possessed all the qualities we have sketched above and possessed by him in full measure. In fact, he was the only perfect man that ever lived. I hope to show that the combination of love, responsibility, authority, and faithfulness that Jesus displayed in his earthly ministry, are also displayed towards his church as he ministers as the risen Lord to her – setting a bench-mark for the Christian husband.

While these qualities are not exclusively masculine ones, Jesus Christ was nevertheless expressing perfect manhood by exercising them. It follows that any Christian man with a role to fulfil for his heavenly Father – in our case that of a Christian husband – will want to emulate his Saviour and strive to attain these same qualities.

---

[1] Matthew 1:18
[2] John 2:1-11
[3] For example: John 19:26
[4] For example John 15:9
[5] John 4:54
[6] Matthew 12:39
[7] 2 Corinthians 8:9; Philippians 2:6-11
[8] Matthew 14:13-21
[9] John 2:15
[10] Matthew 4:18-22
[11] John 19:30

6
Jesus Christ and the Church

After the crucifixion came the resurrection and the ascension, when the risen Lord Jesus Christ went back to heaven to be with the Father.[1] He is now enthroned in heaven at the Father's right hand, where he intercedes for the church and watches over it.[2] He is waiting for the climax of history when he will come to earth again, gather together all believers throughout the ages, and take them to their eternal and glorious home – the place that Jesus has prepared for them. We are told: 'For the Lord himself will come down from heaven, with a loud command, with the voice of the archangel and with the trumpet call of God, and the dead in Christ will rise first. After that, we who are still alive and are left will be caught up together with them in the clouds to meet the Lord in the air. And so we will be with the Lord forever' (1 Thessalonians 4:16-17).

What has all this to do with our subject? A great deal, for this church, which Christ has redeemed and over which he now delights and watches, will one day be his bride!

Jesus describes himself as a bridegroom in the New Testament,[3] and in Revelation chapters 19 to 22 the church at the end of the age is pictured as the bride, being presented to her Bridegroom, the Lord Jesus Christ. Those who know their Old Testaments will not be surprised by this. Many times there God describes himself as a bridegroom, and believers within Old Testament Israel as his bride.

In the letter to the Ephesians the apostle Paul directly compares the husband to Christ, and the wife to his church: 'Husbands, love your wives, just as Christ loved the church and gave himself up for her and to present her to himself as a radiant church, without stain or wrinkle or any other blemish, but holy and blameless. In this same way, husbands ought to love their wives as their own bodies. He who loves his wife loves himself...For this reason a man will leave his father and mother and be united to his wife, and the two will become one flesh. This is a profound mystery--but I am talking about Christ and the church' (Ephesians 5:25-32).

We are specifically told that when a man and woman are joined together in marriage they become like Christ and the church. This is indeed a mystery, but one that provides a key to how we are to understand marriage. In some way a Christian marriage reflects the relationship between Christ and the church.

Jesus Christ the role model

The importance of these verses in Ephesians cannot be over-stressed. Much flows from it that bears upon our subject. The Bible is not often prescriptive about the do's and don't's of marriage – but this passage teaches us *principles* that, if applied, will profoundly affect how we see the relationship of a husband to his wife.

This gives substance to my claim that we can say with some certainty what it means to be a Christian husband. Without having to look further, we have a role model for the husband in our Lord Jesus Christ – a husband is to behave towards his wife as Christ does to his church.

The church's heavenly bridegroom

In the preceding chapter we saw how Jesus Christ related to individual believers and people in general during his earthly ministry. So how does the Saviour relate to his 'bride', the church, now that he has ascended to his Father?

We saw what sort of man Jesus was on earth but has that changed now that he watches over his church from heaven? Does he display the same qualities now he is the Lord in heaven?

If we know the answers to these questions, then we can begin to apply this teaching to the Christian husband, for (as Ephesians makes clear) the relationship of husband to wife should mirror that between Christ and his church.

The earthly Jesus loved, took responsibility, had authority, and was faithful to his friends and to his God-given mission. Ephesians 5 shows us that nothing has changed, for our Lord in heaven does all these things today.

A saviour who loves the church

We read that 'Christ loved the church and gave himself for it' (Ephesians 5:25). Love was the motive behind the greatest rescue plan of all time, Christ's coming to earth to save the church. We read of the Father's love in John 3:16, 'God so loved the world that he gave his one and only Son, that whoever believes in him shall not perish but have eternal life.'

This should not surprise us, for Christ is the perfect expression of the Father. The love that the Father has, the Son has also.

This divine love was not based on short term emotion, an idealised view of humanity, or on the hope of some pay-back. It was a pure love – altruistic, realistic, compassionate, action-based love that cost our Lord dearly. Jesus sought the church and gave himself for her (Luke 19:10; Galatians 1:4).

He did not come to earth and happen to find a lost people, he loved his church long before he embarked on his great mission – indeed, before time began (2 Tim. 1:9). The decision to come was made in heaven.[4]

Back in heaven now he waits for that time, known only to the Father,[5] when he will gather up the object of his love and take her home. Our heavenly Lord loves his church.

A saviour who takes responsibility for the church

The Lord Jesus Christ is not only the 'builder' of his church, he is its guardian and shepherd (Matthew 16:18; John 10:14-30). He has made her preservation and welfare his personal responsibility (John 14:2).

We are told Jesus is preparing a place for us, 'In my Father's house are many rooms; if it were not so, I would have told you. I am going there to prepare a place for you' (John 14:12).

The church is secure in his hands.[6] Throughout the ages he will nurture her, provide for her, and give her eternal security.[7] The gates of Hades will not prevail against her. [8] The church will be presented to our Lord at the end of time blameless and spotless – because he has taken our blame and cleansed our defilement.[9] Nothing was too much trouble for him to secure the church's redemption, as we see in the gospel narratives and supremely at the cross.[10]

He prayed to the Father to secure our future: 'Father, I want those you have given me to be with me where I am, and to see my glory, the glory you have given me because you loved me before the creation of the world' (John 17:24).

Our risen Lord continues to take responsibility for his church.

A saviour who has authority over the church

Ephesians 1:22 tells us that God 'has put all things under [Christ's] feet, and gave him to be head over all things to the church, which is his body'. Again, Colossians 1:18 says, 'He is the head of the body', while Ephesians 4:15-16 develops the same theme.

Whatever else this means, it means that Christ exercises authority over the church – he is its Head, its Leader and its Lord. If we are true to Christ we will as believers accept his Word, as it is revealed to us in the Scriptures.[11]

Jesus says 'If you love me, you will obey what I command' (John 14:15). It is clear from John's gospel and elsewhere that his 'commands' are to be found in the Bible. Only those who hear his sayings and obey them, are building on the Rock (Matthew 7:24-29)!

Our glorified Saviour looks to his church to be obedient to his Word.

A saviour who is faithful to the church

Only by coming to the Saviour do we know the true God. No one comes to the Father except by the Lord Jesus Christ.[12] And all who so come find that Christ is faithful to his church and to his people – he will neither leave them nor forsake them (Hebrews 13:5-6).

Consider some of the New Testament statements about the faithfulness of God.

Right at the beginning of our Christian life we are told 'If we confess our sins, he is faithful and just and will forgive us our sins and purify us from all unrighteousness' (1 John 1:9).

The apostle Paul tells us in his first letter to the Thessalonians that Jesus will then keep believers blameless – 'The one who calls you is faithful and he will do it' (1 Thessalonians 5:24) and in his second letter that 'the Lord is faithful, and he will strengthen and protect you from the evil one' (2 Thessalonians 3:3).

In his letter to Timothy we are told the Lord's faithfulness reaches out to us even when we are faithless – 'if we are faithless, he will remain faithful, for he cannot disown himself' (2 Timothy 2:13).

The apostle John tells us in the closing pages of the Bible, as he catches a glimpse into heaven, that Jesus is called 'Faithful and True' (Revelation 19:11).

Jesus Christ is faithful to his church.

Our responsibility

So we see our Saviour is as he was on earth. He loves the church. He takes responsibility for her. Having sought her out he takes responsibility even now for keeping her safe. He has authority over the church through his Word; he is faithful to her and will not let her down. The same should be true of a husband's loving care towards his wife.

Some might object and say how can such a mundane thing as married life, with all its problems, ups and downs, tedium and care, possibly reflect such an exalted relationship as that between Christ and his church?

But that is exactly what it should do, for – looked at the other way around – marriage is God's picture to help us grasp the heavenly reality of the union between Christ and the church.

It is the responsibility of married Christians, therefore, to see that the picture is displayed to the best of their ability within their own marriage, as an example to God's people and a witness to our fallen world. Our marriages should be a testimony to the mercy and benevolence of Christ towards redeemed sinners – and of their response to his saving love.

In the four following chapters I hope to show how a Christian husband might fulfil his fourfold responsibility to relate to his wife in ways that reflect Christ's love for the church. We shall consider in turn how the husband is to love, to take responsibility, to have authority, and to be faithful.

---

[1] Acts 1:9
[2] Hebrews 8:1,2
[3] For example Matthew 25
[4] Romans 8:29,30
[5] Matthew 24:36
[6] John 14:2,3
[7] John 14:2,3
[8] Matthew 16:18
[9] Ephesians 5:27
[10] John 12:27
[11] 2 Timothy 3:16,17
[12] John 14:6

7
To Love

God is love

We saw in the previous chapter that the relationship of husband to wife should mirror that between Christ and his church – a relationship of love, responsibility, authority and faithfulness. We now begin to explore and apply these different aspects, beginning in this chapter with love.

> Dear friends, let us love one another, for love comes from God. Everyone who loves has been born of God and knows God. Whoever does not love does not know God, because God is love. This is how God showed his love among us: He sent his one and only Son into the world that we might live through him. This is love: not that we loved God, but that he loved us and sent his Son as an atoning sacrifice for our sins. Dear friends, since God so loved us, we also ought to love one another. No one has ever seen God; but if we love one another, God lives in us and his love is made complete in us (1 John 4:7-12).

The capacity to love is God's gift to men and women. Indeed, when man truly loves he is reflecting in his own life the chief attribute of God. When a young man asked Jesus which is the greatest commandment of all, he replied 'to love the Lord our God with all our heart, soul and strength'. He further said that the second greatest commandment is that we should love our neighbour as we love ourselves.[1]

But what is love?

The much used word 'love' has different meanings according to its context – and can mean different things to different people even when used in the same context. 'Love' can describe the loftiest emotion known to man, and a liking for cream buns! It is used to describe a mother's feeling for her newborn child, a patriot's attachment to his country of birth, and the prospect of a warm bath.

In the context of human relationships, most would agree that love includes affection, fondness, positive feelings and concern for another person. Yet, somehow, we believe it is more than these things.

Love is often a mixture of emotions. Strangely, you can love somebody you do not find specially attractive – someone you might not want to be with all the time or even much of the time. One only has to think of a cantankerous elderly relative to see the truth of this.

Romantic love

In the context of marriage people are usually talking about romantic love. Romantic love *does* find the object of its attraction desirable – highly so. A person who loves in this way wants to be close to the object of his or her affections. Romantic love includes an erotic element and the prospect of the fulfilment of such desires, but also involves many other dimensions.

So might an acceptable definition of romantic love be 'a deep and enduring feeling of affection, fondness and sexual desire? If we accept this as a working definition we immediately see a difficulty – romantic love is a mixed and complex emotion. Feelings of affection are mingled with sexual desire, with all its possible ramifications. And what is being 'in love'; is this a different emotion or more of the same?

Being in love

Is 'being in love' with someone different from simply loving them? Most would say it is. 'Being in love' describes a condition when our feelings for another (feelings which we have labelled romantic love) run so high that we are almost swept away by them.

At such a time, nothing done for the loved one seems too much trouble. No happiness can compare with the way we feel when we are with that person. It is a time when we idealise the object of our love and see no wrong, weakness or flaw in them.

These emotions are real – they are not a figment of our imagination; however, we need to ask two questions:

- Is this powerful feeling that one person can have for another – being in love – what the Bible means when it uses the word 'love'?
- Can such emotions be a secure basis for marriage?

The answer to both these questions, I believe, is no. The NIV uses the expression 'in love' four times, describing Jacob as being in love with Rachel,[2] Samson with Delilah,[3] Michal with David,[4] and Amnon with Tamar.[5]

Jacob's love for Rachel proved to be enduring. Michal's love for David seemed genuine but she ended up despising him[8], Samson's love for Delilah led to his capture by the Philistines and Amnon's love for Tamar made him rape her. After which we read: 'Then Amnon hated her with intense hatred. In fact, he hated her more than he had loved her. Amnon said to her, "Get up and get out!"' (2 Samuel 13:5).

So the track record for being 'in love' is not a good one, biblically speaking. We have a 50% failure rate at least, which is about the same as the current UK divorce rate.

I am not saying that such an emotion as 'being in love' does not exist, for the Bible describes it. But I am saying that such an emotion can be transitory and fickle. It is not a firm basis for marriage, and certainly not the *biblical* basis, as we shall see.

It is possible to 'fall in love' with someone who is not your spouse. If being in love is a proper basis for a relationship – and was the basis for your marriage – what is now to stop you forming a relationship with that new person?

If being 'in love' is the overriding criterion it follows that if one ceases to be 'in love' then the relationship and the marriage are over. This is often the justification offered for extra-marital affairs and divorce, yet (despite today's freewheeling attitude on sexual matters) these are disapproved of by the vast majority of married couples.

Love in the Bible

First let us look to see how the Bible uses the word 'love'. There are more than 200 verses in the New Testament alone that contain the words 'love', loves' or 'loved', but there are only three passages that refer to love between a man and a woman!

Ephesians 5:25-33:

> Husbands, love your wives, just as Christ loved the church and gave himself up for her to make her holy, cleansing her by the washing with water through the word, and to present her to himself as a radiant church, without stain or wrinkle or any other blemish, but holy and blameless. In this same way, husbands ought to love their wives as their own bodies. He who loves his wife loves himself. After all, no one ever hated his own body, but he feeds and cares for it, just as Christ does the church– for we are members of his body. "For this reason a man will leave his father and mother and be united to his wife, and the two will become one flesh." This is a profound mystery--but I am talking about Christ and the church. However, each one of you also must love his wife as he loves himself, and the wife must respect her husband.

Mark 12:28-30:

> One of the teachers of the law came and heard them debating. Noticing that Jesus had given them a good answer, he asked him, "Of all the commandments, which is the most important?" "The most important one," answered Jesus, "is this: `Hear, O Israel, the Lord our God, the Lord is one. Love the Lord your God with all your heart and with all your soul and with all your mind and with all your strength.' The second is this: `Love your neighbor as yourself.' There is no commandment greater than these."

Colossians 3:19:

> Husbands, love your wives and do not be harsh with them.

Titus 2:4:

> Then they [the older women] can train the younger women to love their husbands and children.

Straight away we see that 'love' is used as a verb (an 'action word') rather than as a word denoting an emotional state. We are given a command – to love!

A commanded love

So what *sort* of love is commanded? The best known Bible passage about love, and one that is used in many marriage services, is 1 Corinthians 13:

> If I speak in the tongues of men and of angels, but have not love, I am only a resounding gong or a clanging cymbal. If I have the gift of prophecy and can fathom all mysteries and all knowledge, and if I have a faith that can move mountains, but have not love, I am nothing. If I give all I possess to the poor and surrender my body to the flames, but have not love, I gain nothing.
>
> Love is patient, love is kind. It does not envy, it does not boast, it is not proud. It is not rude, it is not self-seeking, it is not easily angered, it keeps no record of wrongs. Love does not delight in evil but rejoices with the truth. It always protects, always trusts, always hopes, always perseveres.
>
> Love never fails. But where there are prophecies, they will cease; where there are tongues, they will be stilled; where there is knowledge, it will pass away. For we know in part and we prophesy in part, but when perfection comes, the imperfect disappears. When I was a child, I talked like a child, I thought like a child, I reasoned like a child. When I became a man, I put childish ways behind me. Now we

> see but a poor reflection as in a mirror; then we shall see face to face. Now I know in part; then I shall know fully, even as I am fully known. And now these three remain: faith, hope and love. But the greatest of these is love [Note: 'love' is rendered 'charity' in the older King James Version of the Bible].

Although this passage is not talking specifically about the love of a husband for his wife, the Greek word used for love (*agapao*[6]) is the same as that used in Ephesians 5:25, where we are told: 'Husbands, love your wives, just as Christ loved the church and gave himself up for her.'

In 1 Corinthians 13 we see that the emphasis is on action rather than emotion. So when the Bible commands us to love we are not primarily commanded to *feel* something but to *do* something. Although love *is* an emotion, the focus in our passage is on actions rather than emotions.

Thus we see from the passage that love:

Positively	**Negatively**
Acts patiently	Does not envy
Behaves in a kindly manner	Does not boast
Rejoices in the truth	Is not proud
Always protects	Is not rude
Always trusts	Is not self-seeking
Always hopes	Is not easily angered
Always perseveres	Does not keep a record of wrongs
	Does not delight in evil

In other words, a loving person is one who is patient, kind, truthful, protective and so on, towards the person they love – and indeed with people in general. An unloving person, by contrast, is boastful, envious, proud, etc.

So here we have a good test. Do we claim to love somebody? Then let's see how we interact with them. Which of the above lists predominates in our relationship with that person?

It is not difficult to see in some boy-girl relationships many of the negative traits listed above – such as boastfulness and selfishness. The Bible says that this is not love – it is something else.

This is not the only area in which the Bible places importance on actions rather than feelings. James says a similar thing about faith (James 2:20-26). Of course, as Christians we do not believe we get to heaven by doing things – but James is pointing out that if our 'faith' produces no good actions, it is not the genuine article.

Similarly, biblical love always manifests itself in the positive actions listed in 1 Corinthians 13, whether the relationship has a sexual dimension (as in marriage) or not (as in loving our fellow Christians). 1 Corinthians 13 is the litmus test of our emotions.

Certainly, if we consider as our prime example, the love Jesus showed in his earthly ministry and the love he now shows for his church, we see an all-positive, action-based love.

To love our neighbour

Husbands are not only to love their wives, but we all must love our neighbours:

> One of the teachers of the law came and heard them debating. Noticing that Jesus had given them a good answer, he asked him, "Of all the commandments, which is the most important?" "The most important one," answered Jesus, "is this: `Hear, O Israel, the Lord our God, the Lord is one. Love the Lord your God with all your heart and with all your soul and with all your mind and with all your strength.' The second is this: `Love your neighbor as yourself.' There is no commandment greater than these." (Mark 12:28-30)

Jesus says that we are to love our neighbour *as ourselves.* It is precisely this terminology that Paul uses in Ephesians 5, telling a husband to love his wife *as himself*, or as his own body.

What love is this?

In what way do we love ourselves? A psychologically healthy person has something we call 'self respect' – a regard for himself and his own well being. Biblical teaching is saying that we should apply the same principle in dealing with our neighbour and our wife. Show them the same respect and regard for their well being as you would want for yourself.

What *do* we want for ourselves? Happiness, fulfilment, security, respect? In that case a loving person will try to see, as far as it lies in his power, that his wife or his neighbour will experience those same things. Such a person will act in a loving and empathising way to others.

A romantic love without empathy is merely adoration or lust – something to please ourselves. A person on the receiving end of such a 'love' may experience no benefit from it at all! Jesus' love for us was an empathic, action-based love. He saw our need and came to meet it at the cross.

Love in marriage

How do we apply this teaching to marriage? For a husband to show love to his wife he should do his best to see that she has no less than he wants for himself. Just as we take care of ourselves and want good things to happen to us, so also we should want the same for our wives. With this approach the Christian husband's motivation will be first to please the Lord and then, in doing so, to please his wife. This is biblical love, empathetic love, love based in action.

Immediately we can see a difference between this and a love that is primarily emotional or that majors on sexual desire. A love based entirely on emotion may lead to action, but it will be action of a selfish rather than an altruistic kind – and may well give rise to a negative experience for the object of such 'love'.

In any case, actions based entirely on emotion can be fickle and short-lived. You see a starving puppy on television and send a donation to the RSPCA. Then the image fades, and with it goes your commitment to starving puppies! In contrast, biblical love springs not primarily from short-lived emotions but from the emotions and the will acting together.

A husband seeking to act in a biblical manner wants his wife to have what he himself wants – that is the nature of his relationship with her. He has taken her as his 'church', he has a duty to her, and he wants the best for her. God in his wisdom has made this duty pleasurable for the man. He finds his wife attractive and good company! Just as eating is necessary to survive (God has also made it pleasurable), so he makes loving our wives a pleasurable duty to fulfil. A husband's motivation should be love and duty, for acting together the one is a catalyst for the other.

Love a duty?

To link love with duty in this way may unsettle many people. Romantic fiction has done much to elevate the emotional state of being 'in love' as the essential ingredient of every boy–girl relationship and the sole reason for any marriage – or even any affair.

For many, their personal emotional pleasure is all important. They speak as if it has become one of our 'human rights' to give free expression to our emotions. It is difficult for us to change people's mindset on this. I am not saying that such an emotion as 'being in love' does not exist – it clearly does. But the fact that the Bible urges us to love, and then describes what love *is* in terms of actions, tells us that love is something we *do*, not just something we experience.

Duty and love together

A locomotive is enormously powerful. For that power to be effective it has to be transmitted through the wheels onto a track. Its great power is then converted into great usefulness as it powers the train along. If that power was not so harnessed there would be danger of great destruction.

So it is with our emotions. They are there, real, and powerful, but they need to be channelled along God-given pathways. Then we will experience the personal fulfilment that God would wish us to have. Such channelled energy can produce much good. But powerful emotions untamed by duty can cause much harm - we see some of it in our society today. Our emotions are important, they are God given. They should not define the direction of a marriage relationship any more than a locomotive defines the direction of the train. The roles and responsibilities guide a marriage, as do the tracks for a train.

A virtuous circle

Let's go back to our list in 1 Corinthians 13. In so many relationships we see a vicious circle with 'tit for tat' retaliations as things go from bad to worse. The husband feels aggrieved at some (perhaps unintentional) comment or act by his wife, and he responds with an unkind comment or act. She in turn snaps back – and so on as it spirals down. Instead, in the Christian marriage, each should try to outdo the other in making life better for their partner.

The husband, if we look at our list, is not to be self seeking, nor easily angered, and he is not to keep a record of wrongs. Rather he is to be patient, kind, protecting and trusting – and to persevere in these things.

Jesus loved his church even when it was unlovely. He was proactive in love. He did not wait for us to express love to him.

A Christian husband, if he is to model himself on his Saviour, should take the initiative in loving acts towards his wife, to initiate not a vicious circle – but a 'virtuous circle'. Here loving acts by the husband cause the wife to imitate with similar loving acts to her husband, each responding to the other in a positive loving way.

I remember in our first year of marriage I was with my wife at our pastor's house. I was engaged in conversation with a friend but behind me I could overhear another conversation.

My wife (Lois) was saying to the pastor's wife (Helen) that she so disliked trying to sort out my socks when they had been through the washer that she just stuck them all back in my drawer afterwards and let me deal with them. To which Helen replied with some surprise – 'Really! I thought you would like to do that job for your husband.'

Later in the week I noticed in my sock drawer - which previously I had never paid any particular attention to, and certainly had not noticed what a great jumble of odd socks it had become – that all my socks were neatly matched up.

What do you think my reaction was when Lois later asked me to go to the shops for something? Like many men 'retail therapy' passes me by. I readily volunteered.

This was my wife's initiative after some wise and godly counsel from an older married woman. It made a bigger impact for me on our marriage than any single sermon I have heard or book I have read.

Jesus took an initiative with us when he left the splendour of heaven that if we thought about it should cause our minds to reel. Is it really so difficult for a Christian husband to emulate him in some ever so small way and initiate loving acts of kindness to his wife?

A love language

Of course it is no good initiating a loving act if that loving act is buying your wife two tickets to the football match when you know she does not like football. No, the husband is to do these things 'according to knowledge' (1 Peter 3:7, KJV): 'Likewise, ye husbands, dwell with them according to knowledge, giving honour unto the wife, as unto the weaker vessel, and as being heirs together of the grace of life; that your prayers be not hindered.'

In other words a husband should look to be knowledgeable about his wife's needs and preferences — and to act accordingly. We are all different. We all have different likes and dislikes, needs and wants.

The husband should take the trouble to find out what makes his wife happy. He should find, in the terms of another author, his wife's 'language of love'.[7]

Part of the genius of God's creation is diversity. All men and women share certain characteristics but then within that range we differ widely. It would be intolerable if this were not the case.

In the *Five Love Languages* Gary Chapman suggests that we have five different areas of our lives in which we can give or receive loving acts, and the relative importance of these areas differ widely between different people.

For example, some wives will want to see a demonstration of their husband's love by him sending them flowers and cards – in other words, tokens of affection - at the expected time (birthdays and anniversaries) as well as spontaneous expressions of the same. If I did this my wife might think there was something wrong. But for some women it is undoubtedly important.

Others will want time together, others a tender word, still others a thoughtful act done unbidden – and so on.

These sorts of thoughtful acts are not the substance of the marriage but by putting these things into practice a husband is showing an empathy with his wife. He shows that he is aware she needs certain things from him and he is prepared to make the effort to please her in that area.

By so doing he shows what he feels in tangible deeds - often not involving much sacrifice from himself. My own observation is that men are not so good at this. We will work hard to provide a home and get many of the 'big' things right, but not do the smaller things that we would do if we were really acting towards our wives 'according to knowledge'.

Also notice in our passage above 'giving honour', or as it is in the NIV, 'respect'. The Greek word can be translated as 'value'.

A husband is to put special value on his wife. He is to treat her as something precious, which she is in and of herself. But when we think that, according to the apostle Paul in Ephesians, she is as the church is to our Lord, then surely we should be prepared to go the extra mile as he did for us.

A lasting love

In a marriage where the husband takes as his example the Lord Jesus Christ, loves his wife as himself, loves according to his duty with acts of the will, initiates loving acts, loves according to his increasing knowledge of his wife, takes into account the 'love language' of his wife, positive emotions to each other will grow and develop – emotions that will last and deepen over the years.

In this way the 'in love' euphoria that we may experience, is built into something more lasting – a marriage where a husband loves his wife.

---

[1] Mark 12:28-34

[2] Genesis 29:18

[3] Judges 16:4

[4] 1 Samuel 18:20

[5] 2 Samuel 13:1

[6] *Agapao* means a giving, self-sacrificing love

[7] Gary Chapman, *The Five Love Languages* (Chicago: Moody, 1996).

8
To Take Responsibility

Jesus Christ and his church

Although Jesus Christ enjoyed all the splendours of heaven, he left his heavenly home to come to our world, to seek and save that which was lost. He came for his church. He then lived his life for her, teaching by Word and example what he expected from her. He then went back to heaven and is even now preparing a glorious heavenly home for her eternal rest. Jesus has told us that no believer will be lost.[1] He *took responsibility* for the task that God sent him to do, and he is holding those who believe safe in his hands.

No husband can hope to emulate the Lord Jesus Christ and the great work the Father sent him to do – but if the husband is in any doubt about the nuance or practical outworking of any Bible teaching, then he can do no better than consider what Jesus himself did, and continues to do, for his church. As we have seen, that is the Bible picture: as Jesus is to the church so a husband should be to his wife.[2]

To take responsibility

Jesus Christ is Head of his church. No Christian should be in doubt about that.

Ephesians 5:23 says: 'For the husband is the head of the wife as Christ is the head of the church, his body, of which he is the Saviour.'

But what does it mean that the husband is 'head of the wife'? Some who support the feminist movement in the church dispute whether the word 'head' carries with it any notion of authority or responsibility. I think this has been well answered by John Piper and Wayne Grudem in *Recovering Biblical Manhood and Womanhood: A Response to Evangelical Feminism.* But whatever the etymology of the actual word there is, there is a direct comparison in our verse here between the husband being head of the wife and Christ being head of the church. Surely, Christ's headship of the church carries with it authority (the subject of our next chapter) and responsibility. If as Christians we reject this we are rejecting the Saviour. We are told that God raised Christ...

> and seated him at his right hand in the heavenly realms, far above all rule and authority, power and dominion, and every title that can be given, not only in the present age but also in the one to come. And God placed all things under his feet and appointed him to be head over everything for the church (Ephesians 1:20-21).

This notion of authority and responsibility must carry through to the husband's role: otherwise the comparison in Ephesians 5:23 would be meaningless.

On Judgement Day will not God call husbands to account over this matter? We have seen how Adam was in a leadership position in his relationship with Eve and was held accountable by God. Also we saw how God related to men and gave then special responsibilities throughout the Old Testament era. Furthermore, we have the powerful picture of Christ and the church. All these things must give clear indications that he expects the husband to take a special responsibility in a Christian marriage.

This is entirely in keeping with the husband's role model - our Lord Jesus Christ. It would indeed be an anomaly if the husband had no special responsibility for his wife.

But what does this mean in practice?

I do not think this means that if anything goes wrong, the husband is automatically to blame. But if a ship hits the rocks the first person to be interviewed is the captain! If the captain has not done what is necessary to secure the safety of his ship he will be held to account.

In the same way, the husband should ensure that things are done properly – according to the 'rule book'. Only *his* rule book is not some seafarer's manual or ship owner's guide, but the Bible.

The Christian husband will try to ensure that there is a framework in place for the marriage to be conducted on a biblical basis and will take responsibility for seeing that, as far as humanly possible, the marriage works along these lines.

For the captain of a ship, the safety of the passengers and crew is his foremost responsibility.

So a husband should ensure his wife and family are secure in all areas of life – physically, emotionally and spiritually. You would not be happy if on a ship you were swept overboard through a gap in the handrail only to be told by the captain that that bit of the boat was not his responsibility. Or if you ended up at the wrong destination only to be told that navigation was not his strong point. As a passenger on his ship the captain owes you a complete duty of care.

If the picture of Christ and the church means anything, surely a husband owes a duty of care to his wife. She needs to be secure.

Secure in or from what? Perhaps, as we have discussed, a wife's security needs may vary from one person to another. An empathising husband will look to see what his wife actually wants and needs.

For example, most women want to feel secure financially, in their own home, emotionally and spiritually, but the emphasis that different women put on each of these things will vary. But if the husband is going to be true to his task, all these areas should surely be on his agenda.

Let us consider specific examples.

Four Specific Examples

Let's look then at some specific Bible teaching about taking responsibility and the way it might be applied in a modern day Christian marriage:

A husband should provide a home for his wife

> In my Father's house are many rooms; if it were not so, I would have told you. I am going there to prepare a place for you. And if I go and prepare a place for you, I will come back and take you to be with me that you also may be where I am (John 14:22).

Jesus has provided a heavenly home for believers; is it not a primary responsibility of the husband to provide an earthly home for his wife?

To feel secure in a good home fulfils an important psychological need for many women. This does not mean that he should rush out and buy a house and present it to his wife as a 'done deal'. But it should be uppermost in his thoughts that it is his responsibility to house his family. He should not have taken a wife without at least having had a plan. The man, we are told, is to leave his father and mother and be united to his wife.[4] Leaving one home suggests finding another. In consultation with his wife it should be his initiative that drives the agenda in finding somewhere suitable to live.

A husband should endeavour to provide financially for his wife

> If anyone does not provide for his relatives, and especially for his immediate family, he has denied the faith and is worse than an unbeliever (1 Timothy 5:8).

The Bible is clear; those who do not provide for their own family are 'worse than unbelievers'. But what does this mean in practice in our modern society? For example, what if the man cannot earn a living or what if the wife is the higher earner or better at finances?

With the agreement of his wife, a husband might want to give up work for a while — for example, to pursue a course of study. During this temporary period, she takes the responsibility for earning their living. But she should not be put under pressure to do this, and if she finds it too difficult the husband should re-assume the role — otherwise he will not be providing for his own family as 1 Timothy 5 says he should. If he is unable to earn a living for whatever reason then obviously she would want to help out.

There is no reason why a wife should not take up paid employment, but biblically speaking she is free not to do so. Nor does it mean that the wife has to fulfil all the domestic responsibilities – that is something to be agreed by each couple for themselves. If she is better able to control the finances than the husband (and this is not uncommon) then there should be no problem – marriage is a partnership. But she must not undermine the authority of her husband, and he cannot abdicate responsibility for the material well-being of the marriage.

Put it this way. She might be the Chancellor of the Exchequer and he the Prime Minister! If a Prime Minister claimed it was not his fault when the national economy went off course – because he had delegated that task to his Chancellor – he would stand little chance at the next general election. To delegate or share responsibility does not shift the primary responsibility from the husband.

The 'male provider' role might seem out of place in today's modern economy, and I do not deny that there are real difficulties with rising levels of male unemployment. However, all the surveys I have read show that many working women, if they could freely choose, would rather spend more time at home.[3] Moreover most men do not mind financially supporting a wife, but few women are keen on financially supporting a house-husband.

Freed from the responsibility of providing for the family financially, a wife can flourish as the home maker, although I stress again that the Bible nowhere forbids the wife having a career of her own.

A husband should ensure the emotional well being of his wife

Have you ever considered that Jesus Christ could have mounted his great rescue plan – and kept quiet about it? He could have returned to heaven and left us guessing where we fitted in the scheme of things. We would not know until Judgement Day where we stood before a holy God. But God in Christ wanted us to *know* that we could rest in him, that we have an eternal home, that we are secure in him.[4]

Our *knowledge* of security does not affect our security – the only reason for telling us was presumably for our benefit and comfort so that we might know and rejoice. It was not just that God had done something; he wanted us to *know* that he had done it.

So a Christian husband should want his wife to feel secure in the knowledge that he is indeed taking responsibility for her needs.

A husband should look to the spiritual security of his wife

Jesus did not come primarily as an example – he came to execute a spiritual rescue plan, to secure the eternal future of his church. Throughout the Old Testament it was the husband who was held accountable for the family's spiritual life.

No husband can secure his wife's eternal future. Only Christ can do that. But he can ensure that the home has a godly Bible-based life and that the family attends a church that teaches the apostles' doctrine.[5] He should put no stumbling block in his wife's way and do all he can to be a good witness to her, so that his behaviour at home is consistent with the gospel he loves.

To live for his wife

Of course, there are other areas where the husband, who is living with his wife 'according to knowledge', will want to ensure she has peace and emotional well being. But a general rule should be that a husband should live for his wife, as we see from this section of Paul's letter to the Corinthian church:

But a married man is concerned about the affairs of this world-how he can please his wife- and his interests are divided. An unmarried woman or virgin is concerned about the Lord's affairs: Her aim is to be devoted to the Lord in both body and spirit. But a married woman is concerned about the affairs of this world-how she can please her husband (1 Corinthians 7:33).

Of course, this passage raises a different issue, namely, whether it is better not to marry at all. Paul here points out the spiritual advantages of the single state. But it nevertheless shows that in marriage to care for one's spouse is a priority. As Jesus lived and died for the church, a husband's motivation should be to please his wife.

This must, at the very least, mean that a husband cannot live his life as if he was a single man. That old life is to be left behind. Pleasing his wife does not mean he abdicates a leadership role (as we shall see in the next chapter), but rather that his day to day motivation is not 'what I want' but 'what is good for my wife'. His responsibility is to his wife.

What about the husband as a father?

In this book I am primarily addressing the issue of a husband's relationship to his wife, but I think in the context of responsibility it is worth mentioning a husband's responsibilities to children.

A husband has prime responsibility for the children's upbringing

Fathers, do not exasperate your children; instead, bring them up in the training and instruction of the Lord (Ephesians 6:4).

A husband's responsibility includes the welfare and behaviour of any children. In so many homes with children this is left to the wife. However, it is the husband who is to set the standard for what is expected in the home and to see it is maintained. We have seen that the husband is the head of the woman and therefore by definition head of the household. The wife's authority over the children stems from the husband, and he should do nothing to undermine this or abdicate his own responsibility. Too often the woman becomes bread winner, organiser and carer for the children, while the husband evades his responsibility in this area.

In this situation the woman has, perhaps unintentionally but nonetheless effectively, marginalized her husband in the home and the marriage — and many men are content to let this happen. In such a home the husband does not love his wife as Christ loved the church. He is not behaving as a Christian husband. He is not taking responsibility for the marriage and the home of which he is the head.

Broad Shoulders?

What I have given above are just examples. I do not wish to be dogmatic, because the Bible itself is not prescriptive.

But whatever your views on the practical matters mentioned above, the role of the Christian husband must surely mean his thoughts are constantly towards his wife and her well-being.

The role relationship is clear in our picture of Christ and the church. The role model for the husband is not a shadowy theoretical concept, but the manly, compassionate Jesus of the Gospel narratives and the 'great high priest' of our gospel era. Christ's relationship with the church is clear. It is up to the Christian husband to accept the challenge and get on with his job.

Maybe some of the things I have mentioned are not fashionable, but all too often a modern wife finds herself going out to work, and then comes home to all the domestic responsibilities, including the care and discipline of the children. Such a wife has let the husband off the hook. She has allowed him to abdicate responsibility for the home. However, if a husband fulfils the duties implied by his role, his wife will experience the personal security that will enable her to flourish as a woman and a wife.

Sadly much of the literature and talk surrounding marriage today tends to blur the roles of husband and wife, giving the impression that the husband has no special responsibilities. Melanie Philips does not write from a specifically Christian perspective but her book, *The Feminisation of Modern Britain*, points out that this myth is exploded as soon as the marriage falls apart. The man is then pursued by the courts or the Child Support Agency to fulfil his financial responsibilities.

God has clearly laid responsibilities on the shoulders of a husband, but lest we complain no man is being asked to sacrifice more than our Lord did. Jesus Christ shouldered the responsibility God gave him. He left heaven and the presence of God the Father, came to earth, and went to Calvary – dying on a cross to fulfil the task he was set. For the joy that was set before him he endured the cross, despising the shame (Hebrews 12:2).

A Christian husband should be prepared to shoulder the responsibilities God asks him to bear – and in doing so, he too will have joy.

---

[1] John 10:28-29

[2] Ephesians 5:25-33

[3] For example National Women and Work survey conducted for BUPA and Top Sante magazine reported in the Warrington Guardian 25 July 2002

[4] For example, Luke 1:4; 5:24

[5] Acts 2:42

9
To Have Authority

Our review of the Old Testament in chapter 5 showed that it was the norm for men to exercise leadership in the home, the state, and in the spiritual life of their families. It does appear that this was God's specific intention, not something that just happened. This did not come about through cultural acceptability, or because men excelled at the exercise of responsibility and authority, but rather because God ordained things that way.

In the New Testament era God no longer deals with Israel as his representative nation on earth, but instead we see the promises made to that nation fulfilled in the church, 'the Israel of God' (Galatians 6:16).

Male leadership in the church

It is clear that in the meetings of the early church, women were never in leadership or authority over men. This has nothing to do with first century culture – the Bible never argues this – but is primarily a theological matter, as we shall see. A woman's intelligence, ability or faithfulness to Christ is never in question.

In fact, in the Gospel narratives it is the men rather than the women who misunderstood Jesus and let him down. Thomas doubted him, Peter failed him, and Judas betrayed him– while Peter, James and John all fell asleep when they should have been watching.

In contrast, it was the women who stayed at the cross when most of the male disciples went into hiding. Women first witnessed the empty tomb and saw the risen Lord. It was they who had to convince the men that this was so and that the men should go and see for themselves. The Apostle Paul lists several women by name in his letter to the Romans and calls them his 'fellow workers'. Women have distinguished themselves in faith, faithfulness, and courage, both in the New Testament records and throughout the history of the church.

But still the Bible is clear that church leadership is to be male. Why? In 1 Timothy 2:12-13 we read: 'I do not permit a woman to teach or to have authority over a man; she must be silent. For Adam was formed first, then Eve. And Adam was not the one deceived; it was the woman who was deceived and became a sinner.'

So Paul gives two reasons, both theological in nature. Firstly, Adam was formed first, then Eve, and as we saw in chapter 4 this natural order arising from the creation of man does imply a certain authority. Secondly, unlike Adam who knew exactly what he was doing, Eve 'was deceived' by Satan. Paul implies that a woman should not assume leadership in the church because, by virtue of her trusting nature, she is more likely to be deceived and led astray.

I am convinced from the context and other parts of the New Testament that Paul is not here saying that women can never speak or pray in church. He is teaching simply that a woman should not hold a teaching or ruling *office* in the church. But the main point is that the principle of male leadership is argued from the creation order and the Fall – not cultural considerations.

We may not like what Paul is saying here, but this is the teaching of God's Word.

Servant leadership

Before we look at male leadership in the home let us consider what we mean by such terms as authority and leadership.

We have seen how Adam and Eve were to be joint rulers of God's creation,[1] but it was Adam who was to have leadership in this and in his relationship with Eve.[2] But what does this mean? Does this God-given leadership mean despotic rule? We have seen many examples of this in history. Sadly, many leap to this negative image when male leadership is spoken of in the context of marriage.

But there are many inspiring leaders in world history. Great leaders become our heroes. Great leaders set the direction and lead by example, serving others as they act for the benefit of those they lead. Think of Winston Churchill, Mahatma Ghandi and Nelson Mandela. Leadership is not a negative thing.

Our images of leadership and authority have perhaps been influenced by the explosion of media coverage over the last 50 years. No longer are the nation's leaders distant figures to be revered, but instead have become victims of all sorts of revelations from the prying media, and objects of fun in satirical and comedy programs on television. From Jasper Carrot's take-off of politicians to Ricky Gervais' merciless portrayal of the boss in 'The Office', it seems nobody in a position of authority is spared.

But godly leadership means taking responsibility for others; to have authority over them for their good or for the achievement of some agreed goal. It often involves the sacrifice of the leader's own needs and comfort for the benefit of those that are being led. The highest government office in the UK is a 'cabinet minister'. But a 'minister' is one who serves. The highest title of all – Prime Minister – really means 'first servant'. Our model of leadership should be that of 'servant leadership'.

The Lord Jesus Christ our example

So where do we go to for such a role model? To the Lord Jesus Christ, of course. He is the husband's role model, both in his earthly life and his heavenly intercession for the church.

We are told that:

> That power is like the working of his mighty strength, which he exerted in Christ when he raised him from the dead and seated him at his right hand in the heavenly realms, far above all rule and authority, power and dominion, and every title that can be given, not only in the present age but also in the one to come. And God placed all things under his feet and appointed him to be head over everything for the Church, which is his body, the fullness of him who fills everything in every way (Ephesians 1:20-23).

While Jesus displayed a manly authority while on earth, his heavenly authority was not generally on display. His authority on earth was exercised quietly and used to achieve his God given mission of securing the salvation of his church. His authority was exercised with restraint and compassion for the benefit of others.

However, John tells us that the detachment of soldiers and officials that came to arrest Jesus in Gethsemane, carrying torches, lanterns and weapons, fell to the ground when he declared 'I am he'.[3] For a moment they caught a glimpse of who Jesus Christ really was and of his heavenly authority.

The rest of this chapter must therefore be read with a clear view of our Saviour in our minds. His was a sacrificial, servant leadership. His undoubted authority was always exercised for the church's benefit, never his own. In Gethsemane he could have called upon ten thousand angels and confounded those that sought to do him harm. Instead he submitted to the cross as a lamb goes to the slaughter.[4] Driven by love he went where no man could follow – and laid down his life for the church.

That is the example set before us.

Male leadership in the home

We cannot get away from it – the Bible expects to see male leadership in the home: 'Wives, submit to your husbands as to the Lord. For the husband is the head of the wife as Christ is the head of the Church, his body, of which he is the Savior. Now as the Church submits to Christ, so also wives should submit to their husbands in everything' (Ephesians 5:22-24).

We have seen in earlier chapters the disastrous consequence of Adam failing to take his proper position in the first family. It is clear that the Fall occurred because Adam did not play his part in that first relationship. Both Adam and Eve rejected God's authority and did what they should not. From this came all the disease, death and suffering that the world has ever known.

We can see from this verse in Ephesians that the New Testament affirms what we saw in the Old Testament, namely, that in the home the husband is to be (and be seen to be) the leader, the one with final authority.

Yet women also have leadership roles. There are numerous examples in contemporary society and in many different fields of endeavour. The Bible places no limit on the role of a woman in secular employment or political office. But in the family God says ultimate leadership should be the prerogative of the husband.

Responsibility and authority go together

Responsibility and authority go together like a horse and carriage. In no sphere of life do we ask a person to take responsibility without giving them the necessary authority. The state has a responsibility to keep our roads safe, but to do so it needs the authority of the police service and the law courts to enforce its legislation. My local library has a responsibility to maintain its stock of books – so if I take my library book back late, it has the authority to fine me.

In virtually all walks of life, responsibility and authority go hand in hand. In Romans 13, Paul says that there is no authority except that which God has established; and that authority is real and capable of being exercised. What this means in the context of any given marriage is up to each couple to decide – preferably before marriage and with an open Bible. If you come to this later in the marriage it will need much discussion and willing submission to God's Word.

Some Objections

Some will object, but I cannot help that – this book is about the Christian husband as described in the Bible. But what are these objections? I believe there are four main ones:[5]

Women are equal to men

The first objection is based on the idea that 'men and women should be equal'. But what does this mean? Does it mean that men and women are 'the same'?

I am tempted to say, 'obviously not'. In the past 30 years some have argued that men and women are 'the same' and it is only stereotyped upbringing in our families that has produced the differences. I think I am right in saying that this 'feminist' view is no longer held by the majority today. Women and men really are different – thank God!

But women *are* equal to men in their standing before God. The Bible is clear about this. Equality and authority are not antithetical. You can be subject to someone in authority but be more than their equal in intelligence, strength, beauty - or any other measure you might choose. It is important to grasp this. Equality and sameness, worth and authority, are quite different things and should not be confused.

Failure to understand this seemingly subtle distinction leads to many needlessly heated debates. Perhaps the problem is that positions of authority in the secular world are generally held by people of greater ability and carry with them greater financial rewards and status. But to carry this thinking into the family or the church is worldly thinking of the worst sort. The highest office in the church was that of apostle – but Peter, Paul and James refer to themselves as servants.[6] Hopefully we will see that the whole concept of a position of leadership and responsibility in the home is about service, not 'lording' over others.

The Bible's teaching was only relevant to the culture of the time

The second objection is that the Scriptures are limited by cultural factors which apply only to the days in which they were written. This is often said, even by Christians who have a high view of the Bible.[7] However the Bible derives its teaching in this area from two main sources.

First, we are told in 1 Corinthians 11:3 that God is the head of Christ: 'Now I want you to realize that the head of every man is Christ, and the head of the woman is man, and the head of Christ is God.'

So there is some sort of hierarchy in the Godhead – yet as orthodox Christians we believe that all members of the Trinity are indeed fully God, in and of themselves. This teaching can be difficult to understand,[8] but nonetheless Paul goes on to compare this arrangement in the Godhead with the headship of man relative to the woman. So he is arguing from the very nature of the unchanging Godhead, not from contemporary culture.

Second, as we saw in 1 Timothy 2:12-14, Paul tells us that the creation order and Eve's role in the fall are significant in the gender roles God assigns us. What greater foundational themes does the Bible contain than the trinity, creation and the Fall?

How could the New Testament authors have made the matter more emphatic or clear? To deny this teaching is, I believe, special pleading by a generation whose thinking is dominated by secular rationalism.

Male authority is open to abuse

The third objection is that male authority is open to abuse. Indeed it is – like all other positions of authority. Do we then have to disband our police force and army, and remove employers and every other authority structure? Obviously life would be impossible if this were to happen.

Abuse can and does occur, but it is the exception that makes the headlines. In my experience, if you give someone genuine authority they often take their task much more seriously, and take greater responsibility for doing it well. Parents, for all practical purposes, have absolute authority over their children – which means that their children are vulnerable. But the vast majority of parents use that authority in a loving and sacrificial way.

A loss of freedom

The fourth and final objection is that the Bible's teaching represents an amazing curtailment of a woman's freedom – some say it is like stepping back in time.

But where does freedom lie ? Imagine there was a move to integrate the UK further into Europe and it was recommended that we should all drive on the right hand side of the road. A referendum is taken but the result is inconclusive. So the government says, choose yourself. Everyone is free to drive on whatever side they like.

Where is freedom then ? One can only imagine the chaos, the deaths and the resultant logjam of traffic. In reality we would not be free to drive at all. And what of the single mother in a high rise flat with two teenage children and an absent father – struggling with a low paid job and the discipline of her recalcitrant children. What freedom does she have?

Let us read what James says in the New Testament: 'But the man who looks intently into the perfect law that gives freedom, and continues to do this, not forgetting what he has heard, but doing it – he will be blessed in what he does' (James 1:25).

The perfect law is the law of God – the Bible. Rather than being restrictive for the woman, a biblical marriage framework allows her freedom to pursue her gifts and explore her role in life within a secure environment.

All the world a stage

I believe the situation can be clarified by a discussion of roles. We are used to playing roles in life. I can be husband, father, son, employee, brother, friend and so on – all in the same day! We are all familiar with having to wear different 'hats' in different situations.

So at home Mary Smith is a wife, mother, friend, neighbour and so on – but then she puts on her uniform and becomes a senior police officer. In that role she has authority, not as Mary Smith but as a Police Superintendent appointed by the state. Her authority in that post is real, but limited to the role of a police officer. She cannot go home and tell her neighbour to get his haircut.

For years I reported to a line manager (the 'boss') at the company where I worked. Were we 'equal'? Yes, in the eyes of God. But did we have equal responsibility or authority (or indeed equal pay)? No, but this did not upset me – in fact I was more than happy with it. I did not think my boss was intrinsically 'superior' to me, although he was vastly more knowledgeable at that time. Also I had no desire to carry his level of responsibility. I was happy doing my job.

Contrast my own (or anybody else's) situation in employment with that of a wife.

When a couple marry the wife effectively appoints a particular man to the office of 'husband'. It is her choice to have a husband – and she chooses the man to fill the role. In that position the husband is to work and live for the well being of his wife. In contrast, my boss was not operating for my benefit – he was working primarily for his own and the company's interests. Nor did I appoint him – he was there when I arrived!

The husband holds his authority, not in himself, but because he occupies the office of husband, an office on which God has bestowed authority. It is the *office* of husband that has the authority, not the person. Mary Smith's husband Mike has no authority over any other woman, unless he holds another 'office' that gives him such authority (for example being the manager at a place of employment). Furthermore it is the woman who has appointed him to occupy the office of husband. He could not have held the post without her express wish.

On the whole, we are comfortable with role relationships in the workplace and the state, but the conversation can get heated when we apply them in the home. In my own employment I had to accept my situation or leave. The wife however does not have the same freedom to come and go (at least in most cultures!).[9] So choosing the right husband is crucial, and not to be left to the vagaries of being 'in love'.

We will return to this in chapter 12 'Getting Married'.

A final example

In his book *Seven Habits of Highly Effective People,*[10] Stephen Covey, who describes himself as a [Christian] 'believer',[11] gives an illustration of marriage in action.

In the hypothetical scenario the husband had promised to take his sons on a fishing trip for their holidays. However his wife wants to use the holiday to visit her ailing mother with her family. In the ensuing argument a reluctant compromise is worked out.

The author suggests a 'middle way' (apparently a Buddhist term) where the couple reach a 'higher unity'. They communicate on a 'higher level' and 'pool their desires' – they 'synergize'. They 'communicate back and forth until they come up with a solution they both feel good about'.

It might indeed be possible to satisfy both requirements. Perhaps there is some good fishing close to the ailing mother's home! But I would not recommend the 'middle way' as a sure way of resolving all the differences that inevitably arise in married life. 'Communicating back and forth' can rapidly become an argument in which each contestant stakes out their own ground.

I believe the Christian way to handle this would have been as follows: There is no argument. The husband knows that he has the final say. So while his wife explains her point of view, instead of concentrating on marshalling his own arguments, he listens carefully to her and all the points she makes. Between them they discuss the matter and finally he makes the decision – based on everything he has heard, and what he believes is best for the family, including and especially, his wife.

She is relaxed about this because she knows her husband is endeavouring to act in her best interests. It is his clear duty. He will have to answer for the way he discharged his role on the judgement day. His role model is Jesus Christ who gave himself for 'her' (the church).

Summing up

What does all this mean in practice in a Christian home in the 21st century? If the husband is to take responsibility he has to have genuine authority. For example, if the wife wants financial security and accepts that the husband is ultimately responsible for providing it, she should not go out and buy an expensive new car without consultation.

Let us imagine that they do discuss it and the husband says that they cannot afford a new car. If she buys it anyway, how can he possibly continue to be responsible for the financial stability of the family? In every relationship, one person ultimately has to defer to the other when there is a disagreement – something inevitable in any long term relationship.

The Bible clarifies this matter by stating that the wife should defer to the husband if no agreement can be found. Ultimately the husband will be held responsible by God himself, so he must have the final decision.

God made us. He knows our hearts. A marriage break up often leaves the woman more vulnerable than the man. She usually has to take responsibility for child care and is less likely than the man to re-marry.[12] The man needs to see his role as a husband as one that carries real responsibility and authority. He will then be more inclined to invest greater effort in his marriage. In such a situation he is far less likely to walk out. A husband should use his authority in the home in a Christ-like way, providing the leadership which God requires of him.

---

[1] Genesis 1:28

[2] Genesis 2:20-23

[3] John 18:2-5

[4] Matthew 26:53

[5] For more discussion about possible objections see chapter 13.

[6] 2 Peter 1:1; Titus 1:1; James 1:1

[7] See for example chapter 11 of *Divorce and Remarriage in the Church* by David Instone-Brewer published by Paternoster Press, 2003.

[8] See an excellent book *The Three are One* by Stuart Olyott Published by Evangelical Press.

[9] The wife can 'dismiss' the husband from that office either by separation or in certain circumstances divorce. See Mark 10:12 qualified by Matthew 19:9. But of course in this situation the wife loses any benefits that the office of husband brought her. See also 1 Corinthians 7.

[10] *Seven Habits of Highly Effective People* by Stephen Covey, p. 271.

[11] Ibid., p. 319.

[12] Centre for Analysis of Social Exclusion London School of Economics May 1998 Kathleen Kiernan and Ganka Mueller.

10
To Be Faithful

A great mystery

> Husbands, love your wives, just as Christ loved the church and gave himself up for her and to present her to himself as a radiant church, without stain or wrinkle or any other blemish, but holy and blameless. In this same way, husbands ought to love their wives as their own bodies. He who loves his wife loves himself...For this reason a man will leave his father and mother and be united to his wife, and the two will become one flesh. This is a profound mystery--but I am talking about Christ and the church (Ephesians 5:25-32).

Returning to this passage we see that sexual intercourse – in which a husband and wife are united physically and become 'one flesh' – is a wonderful and mysterious thing. It is God's idea and designed by him, not only as a means of procreation but to consummate the relationship of companionship between Adam and Eve.[1]

Also, as we have seen, the union of a man and woman in marriage is a picture of what the bible calls the 'wedding supper of the Lamb'[2] – that great day when Christ will return in glory at the end of time and take his church (all true believers) back with him to heaven, to the place he has prepared.

Because sexual intercourse 'foreshadows' the eternal union of Christ with his church, it should clearly only take place within heterosexual marriage. If a man has a casual affair or goes with a prostitute the entire picture is lost – as is the significance of the act itself. All that is left is transitory physical pleasure, not to mention the guilt that often follows. That is why Paul speaks so strongly against unfaithfulness and promiscuity: 'Do you not know that your bodies are members of Christ himself? Shall I then take the members of Christ and unite them with a prostitute? Never! Do you not know that he who unites himself with a prostitute is one with her in body? For it is said, "The two will become one flesh"' (1 Corinthians 6:15-16).

The family

Furthermore, to casualise the sex act undermines one of the three great institutions God gave the world for mankind's benefit – the state, the family and the church.

The family is the building block of every society. Where experiments have been tried to base a community on another model, for example the kibbutz, they have usually failed. It was God's intention that we should all live in families. He sets out the rules for family life quite clearly in the Bible. The basic unit of the family is man and wife, and to bind them together in a unique relationship God gave the gift of sexual intercourse.

The Bible makes it clear that all sin breaks our fellowship with God, but for a man to 'unite himself to a prostitute' is to commit a sin that particularly offends God. It is a sin that degrades the symbol of God's purposes in the plan of salvation and destabilises the family unit. To break the link between sexual intercourse and heterosexual marriage is to break the chain that holds together both the family and, ultimately, society itself.

Reaping the whirlwind

We see from this that the casual use of the sex act by modern society is as far removed from a biblical perspective as it could possible be. To our contemporary society sex is little more than a transitory pleasure; at best a pleasure enjoyed within a relationship but for some not necessarily a hetero-sexual one. Many problems stem from this approach, as we saw in the introduction – including the increasing break up of families, the spread of sexually transmitted diseases, and millions of abortions world wide.

We really have sown the wind and are now reaping the whirlwind. What was intended to picture a profound spiritual truth, and to strengthen a sacred relationship essential to family life, has become destructive of life.

A man's responsibility

Surely no man with a biblical perspective can view sex as a means of short term gratification. He will treat his own body with respect and keep himself for marriage. He will be faithful within marriage, and encourage his wife to maintain that same perspective.

This is primarily a male responsibility. We have often been taught that man is only fulfilling his destiny by propagating his seed as widely as possible. By definition, biological evolution has no moral basis. Evolutionary teaching has swept all before it in our culture, dominating education and the media. It has penetrated every area of life, including the outlook of many of our churches. As a result many accept evolution as a fact – an unseen, unthinking force that is motivating us to survive at all costs.

This world-view has potentially disastrous consequences for any civilised society. Most Christians reject an evolutionary analysis of our origins and stick with the biblical account. Here we read of a loving, purposeful God who created men and women to glorify Him and to reflect something of the Godhead in their own being. In this scheme of things the human race has an exalted role, a moral purpose and accountability to God.

Genesis tells us that Eve's desire would be for her husband.[3] Women not only have a natural sexual desire, they often think that by giving themselves to the man in this way, they are giving and receiving love – so strengthening a God-given relationship.

It is a sad fact that sexual intercourse for the male is often not bound up with the same feelings of love and emotional commitment – sexual gratification predominating.[4] Women are often deceived, therefore, and in this way they are more vulnerable than men.

Workers in the field of teenage pregnancy repeatedly comment that many of these young women have a very low opinion of their early sexual encounters. In contrast to the men the women often say they only had sexual intercourse for emotional reasons, for the giving and receiving of love and affection. Sadly, peer group pressure also plays a strong role. They were not seeking (and did not get) sexual gratification.

It is up to a man to be honest with himself and his partner, and invest the sex act with this God-given perspective. I believe very few women would object to this. It is for the man to take the initiative and show moral integrity. This would surely only enhance his standing in the woman's eyes.

A marriage act

Sexual intercourse is a marriage act and in that context greatly to be enjoyed. The bible's strictures and rules, far from being onerous, are for our long term good and pleasure.

The apostle Paul says the married couple are not to deny each other.[5] This obviously includes the husband. It is one of his duties to ensure that the marriage act happens; that it happens often enough to satisfy his wife; and to take on board the apostle's injunction, that no pleasure is to be denied his wife. The New Testament makes it clear that the marriage bed is 'pure'[6] – in other words, we are not to be ashamed of its pleasures. The marriage act is God's gift jointly to the husband and the wife but (as in the rest of the marriage) the husband has special responsibilities.

It is his responsibility to ensure that this physical side of the relationship is kept alive and exciting – that he 'rejoices in the wife of his youth'[7] and confines this sexual expression to within marriage. The wife of a Christian husband should feel total sexual security and be able to rejoice in it.

Despite 40 years of so-called sexual freedom since the advent of changing social attitudes and the contraceptive pill, most married couples still feel that sexual faithfulness is important. This is particularly true of women. Many today see the bible as outmoded but in this matter, even a cynical and sexually 'liberated' generation must admit it is right up to date.

[1] Genesis 2:20-24

[2] Ephesians 5:31-32; Revelation 19:9

[3] Genesis 3:16

[4] Visiting prostitutes and rape are still largely a male preserve – both activities showing the sex act largely divorced from empathy.

[5] 1 Corinthians 7:5

[6] Hebrews 13:4

[7] Proverbs 5:18

11
Getting Married

Why marry?

> Now for the matters you wrote about: It is good for a man not to marry. But since there is so much immorality, each man should have his own wife, and each woman her own husband. The husband should fulfill his marital duty to his wife, and likewise the wife to her husband. The wife's body does not belong to her alone but also to her husband. In the same way, the husband's body does not belong to him alone but also to his wife. Do not deprive each other except by mutual consent and for a time, so that you may devote yourselves to prayer. Then come together again so that Satan will not tempt you because of your lack of self-control. I say this as a concession, not as a command. I wish that all men were as I am. But each man has his own gift from God; one has this gift, another has that. Now to the unmarried and the widows I say: It is good for them to stay unmarried, as I am. But if they cannot control themselves, they should marry, for it is better to marry than to burn with passion (1 Corinthians 7:1-9).

The apostle Paul, writing to the church at Corinth, tells us it is good to remain single. There is no stigma attached to the single state as far as the bible is concerned. But it is also good to marry.

So there is no command to marry in the bible. Clearly, then, a man should not marry unless he is ready to take on the responsibilities of marriage and is keen to do so.

In times past (and in other cultures today) one reason to marry is to consummate a relationship in a manner acceptable to society. As we see above, this is a valid biblical reason for marriage. But In contemporary Western society there is little pressure on couples to marry in order to enjoy a sexual relationship.

Other biblical reasons for marriage include companionship and mutual comfort (which appears to be why God made Eve for Adam in the first place) and the procreation of children. Children are not the sole purpose of marriage, but it was expected throughout the Old and New Testaments that children would only be born within families, that is, to married couples.

There are many things about which we have no choice. We cannot choose our gender or our parents! Our citizenship is fixed at birth and is difficult to change thereafter. Our circumstances are also mostly determined for us – for example, most people have to work to live. But the major decision whether or not to marry is one that we can make for ourselves. It is a conscious and personal decision, and one that a Christian should make with great care.

Incidentally, having decided to marry, I believe it is right that a man should take the initiative. Christ took the initiative when he sought the church. In the past this responsibility has remained a male preserve – relatively few women would approach a man and ask for a date, let alone propose marriage. Apparently this is no longer the case in modern society!

Ignore this advice

Looking at it from the man's perspective – assuming he is ready to marry – who should he choose, and on what basis?

As to who he chooses, secular literature is awash with advice that usually boils down to one thing – marry the one with whom you are 'in love'. Women are often carried away with this concept. Sadly, even some Christian literature gives being 'in love' as the single most important determinant in choosing a life partner. As we have seen in chapter 8, however, this is not the thinking of the Bible.

The terminology alone should make us wary. We talk about 'falling in love'. The whole point about falling is that we have lost control – specifically, control of our balance. Experience should tell us that we should never base any action on emotion alone, especially when those emotions appear to be out of control. Remember, the action we are talking about here is entering into a contract that could last fifty years or more!

Despite this seemingly obvious caution the prevailing advice remains, 'if you are in love it will be OK'.

Christians are usually advised to 'seek the Lord's will'. If this means seeking what God has revealed in the scriptures about the nature of marriage and the respective roles of husband and wife, I am happy with that. But the implication in some books is that we should seek extra-biblical signs, such as coincidences and strange providences, or rely exclusively on our feelings. I am less than convinced about that kind of advice.

Some biblical advice

For reliable advice we need to turn to the Bible. Here we learn first and foremost that the Christian's intended partner should also be a Christian,[1] for to be 'unequally yoked together with unbelievers' is a recipe for disaster (2 Corinthians 6:14).

The Bible also recognises that for marriage to be considered there will be a strong mutual attraction – a certain 'chemistry' – between the parties concerned (Genesis 29:20). But beyond that it is impossible to be specific. Couples of widely different interests, educational background, temperament etc have successful marriages. Indeed it often seems that, as with magnetism, 'opposites attract' and stay together.

However, in the outworking of the marriage the biblical pattern is clear. The man is to be to his wife what the Lord Jesus Christ is to his bride, the church. For the marriage to work on this basis – the man must ask himself, Do I want to be like Jesus Christ to this woman? Do I want to fulfil all the lifetime responsibilities to her that this entails?

Whatever the chemistry or attraction, if the answer is not 'yes' to both these questions, then the man should not ask the woman to marry him. Marriage for the man means assuming a role and fulfilling it until death brings an end to the marriage. This role, as we have seen, is to love, to take responsibility, to exercise authority and to be faithful. If he is not ready for this he should stay single. And if the man is ready for his role, it should be ascertained that the prospective wife is ready for hers – but that's another book!

What about children ?

Contrary to some Christian viewpoints, the primary purpose of marriage is not to have children.[2] Marriage was ordained principally for the mutual help and companionship of individual men and women in their walk through life. The family does not need children to be complete; this is never taught in the Bible.

However, the Bible is clear that children bring blessing to a family – they are 'a heritage from the Lord ... like arrows in the hand of a warrior...happy is the man who has his quiver full of them' (Psalm 127:3-5). It was God's intention that children should be brought into the world and nurtured by a husband and wife. If a man wants children he will not just be seeking a wife, but also a mother to his children. The same applies, of course, to a woman seeking a father for her children. In addition to the two questions above, the couple also need to discuss carefully their thoughts about having and rearing children – a subject that has far-reaching practical implications, such as whether the wife will be able to pursue a career.

A pre-nuptial agreement

Anyone seeking to counsel a couple about marriage would be wise to encourage the perspectives discussed in this chapter. Less time should be spent talking about 'being in love' or seeking signs or providences in confirmation, and more time on the objective teaching of the Word of God.

'Pre-nuptial agreements' are popular in Hollywood, though still not recognised in British courts. These agreements, signed by a couple before their marriage, outline what should happen should the marriage break up. They usually try to restrict the amount of money that the husband has to pay if there is a separation or divorce.

The Bible effectively contains a pre-nuptial agreement to which Christians contemplating marriage should subscribe. This biblical agreement, however, is not to anticipate the breakdown of the marriage but rather how the marriage is to be kept together and remain alive. It teaches the meaning of marriage, and explains what roles the husband and wife are to fulfil.

The Bible is clear on all the main principles, but it is not prescriptive as to details. It is up to each couple to work out (preferably before they marry) what the general principles of Scripture mean for them personally – and then stick with them!

---

[1] 1 Corinthians 6:14

[2] Genesis 2:18; 1 Corinthians 7:9

12
Some Objections

Although we have now completed our main study of the Christian husband, there are a number of things still to say and a number of conclusions yet to be drawn. In this chapter we consider briefly some possible objections to what I have been saying throughout this book.

Surely we cannot believe the Bible today?

Well, you would probably not have read this far if you really thought that. This is a big subject on its own, and not one we can deal with here because it would require too much space. Suffice it to say that for everyone who dismisses the Bible you will find someone else, equally qualified, thoughtful and intelligent, who believes the Bible is the Word of God, authoritative and relevant in every age. If you want to pursue this matter further, I can suggest a few books for you to read that I have found helpful — such as *Does God believe in atheists?* by John Blanchard, *Is the Bible true?* by Jeffery Sheler and *If I were God I'd make myself clearer* by John Dickson. You will find details of these books in the bibliography under 'apologetics'.

All this man – woman thing is specific to Bible times and cannot be applied today.

This is often said even by some Christians. However, if you look at the verses I have quoted, you will see that the Bible writers do not take their lead from the cultural norms of the day, but from eternal principles grounded in the Trinity, creation and the Fall.

Where is the love and emotion in all this talk about roles and duty?

We looked at this in chapter 8, but I fear that some will not be convinced – especially if they feel that 'personal fulfilment' overrides all other moral or ethical considerations. The weakness of this approach is that sooner or later our personal fulfilment will come into conflict with our neighbour's well being – and where does that leave our Christian duty to love our neighbour as ourselves?

It is not that the Bible dismisses personal fulfilment as of no consequence – on the contrary, it speaks freely about a legitimate love for ourselves. It is rather that the Bible subjects personal freedom to the higher principles of duty and responsibility. Even the Lord Jesus Christ, we read, 'pleased not himself' (Romans 15:3). He gave up the freedom of heaven to take up the cross. Why? Because of love. For him fulfilling this 'duty' was an expression of his love.

Every marriage is different, so you cannot impose the same rigid pattern on every couple.

I would not want to. Each person is unique – that is part of the genius of creation. But there are still principles that apply to all. Think of the human body. No two bodies are identical (even those of 'identical twins') but they all conform to the same blueprint. All have the same 212 bones, the same limbs, the same configuration of facial features. But on this common framework is built a unique body, forming part of our unique soul. The Bible's blueprint for marriage is like a skeleton on which every marriage puts its own flesh – so that each couple can form their own unique and beautiful marriage.

No woman in the 21st century can be expected to obey her husband.

Why not? We are all subject to the authority of others in one way or another in our everyday life. We accept the authority of the State, the authority of our employer, the authority of parents while we are young – even the authority of a sixth-former directing car-parking at the school fete! In all these cases we recognise that the authority to which we submit is acting for our comfort, safely and general good. What is so difficult, therefore, about the authority of a husband in marriage?

So the objection must really reduce to either 1. That there should not be an authority structure in marriage at all, or, 2. If there is, gender should not be the deciding factor.

In practice in most relationships there is one who takes the lead. By definition it is extremely difficult to have two equal independent wills acting in harmony (even the secular State sees the married couple as a unity for many purposes). One or other of the parties must have the final say or takes the lead – even if in subtle ways. The Bible says that there is to be such a 'lead person' in marriage.

Christians accept by faith the things the Bible tells them. And the Bible teaches that in this particular area, gender matters. So ultimately it is question of trusting God's wisdom as it is expressed in God's Word.

Even many non-Christians see the wisdom of this arrangement. In contemporary society, how many wives really want to be the leader in the relationship, and have the final say in their marriage? How many single women really want to go into a marriage knowing that they are going to be the head of the house? A small minority, I would imagine – which further suggests that the biblical pattern is the one God knows is best.

What if the husband does not fulfil his responsibilities but still wants to have authority in the home? What if the husband is not up to being head of the household or a 'servant leader'? What if the wife refuses to obey?

Ultimately, if either partner does not fulfil their role – and no accommodation can be found to resolve the situation – it may become impossible for the couple to live together in peace. In these circumstances the Bible makes it clear that separation is permissible (See 1 Corinthians 7:10).

How can a husband possibly be responsible for everything that happens in the marriage?

I agree that he cannot necessarily ensure that everything works perfectly and that they live happily ever after in married bliss. As we have seen in the case of a ship's captain, the leader of a political party, or the headmaster of a school – when something goes wrong in their organisation they are the first to bear responsibility. Only if they show they could not have foreseen the problem, or truly had control over whatever went wrong, are they absolved from blame.

No marriage is perfect, because *people* are not perfect. But an earnest endeavour to follow the biblical pattern for marriage will be honoured by God, and when problems do arise they will be more readily resolved.

Who today would seriously think of basing their marriage on the guidelines of this book?

Every Christian who believes that the Bible is God's Word believes that God speaks to us in Scripture. But if you reject the Bible's guidelines, what will you use in their place? Once the Bible is set aside there really are no rules to follow. Marriage guidance experts, who base their advice on secular humanism or even 'common sense and experience' really have little to offer. Of course, we should always be willing to learn from the experience of others, whether they are Christians or not, but if they have no authority to rely on, they can only guess at what 'rules' should apply within marriage – if any at all.

This approach leaves each couple to make up their own minds about roles, responsibilities, mutual expectations, guidelines for bringing up children, and so on. This is a daunting and hazardous task and few accomplish it without grief.

Fortunately, in practice, much of what happens in secular marriages today in nominally Christian countries has its roots in biblical teaching inherited from earlier generations. But it is far better to follow the Maker's instructions directly, and they are found only in the Bible!

13
A Conclusion

Despite all the demographic trends and the respectability society now accords to cohabiting, people do still marry! At a recent group interview, my office manger asked the dozen or so young applicants what ten things they most wanted out of life. All the young women said they wanted to marry. Marriage is not for everyone, of course, and single women today can have good independent and financially secure lifestyles. Nevertheless, the institution of marriage is far from dead in our culture. So why is it so resilient?

It is resilient because it was ordained by God. That is the reality underlined in this book. When God created Adam, the man was perfect but alone. Declaring that this loneliness was 'not good' for man, God then made Eve. As a result, men and women still feel the need for this companionship – and many want it in a secure relationship formalised in some way and recognised by family and friends. This is the biblical model. Indeed, many couples still feel the need to marry even after they have been cohabiting for some time and are under no peer, family or financial pressure to do so.

Our main concern in this book, however, has been the specific role of a husband. It is a God-given role and one that man was created to fulfil. As a husband he has been appointed by God to a position of responsibility and authority – yet his role involves a willingness to subordinate his own interests for the greater good of his family. It is a role that gives him recognition in society, respect in the home and release for the masculine characteristics of energy, assertiveness and his protective instinct.

Sadly, we are seeing a new generation of young men who often come from single parent homes (usually single-mother homes) and have no male role-models on which to base their own lives. The potential for further moral and social decline is great. Society has devalued the role of husband, causing some men to vote with their feet and opt for alternative lifestyles. If society and government wants its young men to opt for marriage and family stability in the future they will have to re-evaluate their attitudes to marriage.

In doing so they can have no better pattern than that provided by God himself in the Bible and briefly rehearsed in this small book. If a woman desires a relationship with a man, it is surely best for her to be in a Christian marriage with all that it offers in terms of personal, emotional, financial and sexual security. Within this framework she can offer to her husband all that she has to give, and yet be free to develop as a person, as a woman, and as a wife.

Likewise, the man will find fulfilment as a husband according to God's creation order – a pattern of life in which, like Christ himself, he loves and gives without reserve. This is true manhood and true happiness.

Finally, marriage serves a greater purpose. There are no mistakes with God. He knows the end from the beginning, for he is 'the Alpha and the Omega' (Revelation 22:13). Our heavenly Father knew that men and women would need a Saviour and provided in advance – in marriage – a vivid picture of the role and responsibilities of the Messiah, even Jesus Christ, 'who loved us and gave himself for us' (Galatians 2:20).

When we look at christian marriage we should be able to see mutual concern and affection one for the other. We should see the husband taking responsibility and being faithful to his divinely appointed task, and in turn we should see the complementary submission by his wife, fulfilling with joy her own divinely appointed role as a companion, help-meet and partner.

As we see this picture played out in our lives, and in those of Christian couples we admire, we shall gain increasing understanding of the nature of Christ's relationship to the church. This in turn will enable us to look forward with eagerness to the great consummation of history – when Jesus Christ, having already prepared a place for his bride, will come to take her home and all things will be made new.

We need marriage. God ordained it for our good. The church is encouraged by it, society builds upon it, and those who marry usually benefit from it – especially if they practise it according to the pattern of God's Word.

Men should go to their task, fulfil their destiny, and seek to become the husband that God would have them be.

The world needs men...

who cannot be bought
whose word is their bond
who put character above wealth
who possess opinions and a will
who are larger than their vocations
who do not hesitate to take chances
who will not lose their individuality in a crowd
who will be as honest in small things as in great things
who will make no compromise with wrong
whose ambitions are not confined to their own selfish desires
who will not say 'do it because everybody else does it'
who are true to their friends through good report and evil report in adversity as well as in prosperity
who do not believe that shrewdness, cunning, and hardheadedness are the best qualities for winning success
who are not ashamed or afraid to stand for the truth when it is unpopular
who can say 'no' with emphasis, although the rest of the world says 'yes'

Author unknown

Other *Publications from* Evangelical Press

God's Design for Women

Biblical Womanhood for Today

Women today are encouraged to think they can 'have it all': career success and family fulfilment at the same time. But these external measures of 'success' leave many feeling inadequate. Sharon James shows that every woman has dignity as she has been made in the image of God, and that every woman can find true fulfilment when she understands, enjoys and fulfils her creation design.

Questions for group discussion are provided.

ISBN 0-85234-503-8

Sharon James

God's design for

Women

Biblical Womanhood for today

'written in a compelling, compassionate, down-to-earth style that is immensely readable'
— Grace Magazine

'If you are going to read one book on biblical womanhood this should be it. Sharon James' book is clearly born out of years of study as well as years of experience in a pastoral context.'
— Themelios (International Journal for Theological and Religious Studies Students)

'essential reading for both women and men in our churches'
— Evangelical Times

'Sharon James is a stimulating thinker. We need more of this calibre of Christian writing at a popular level.'
— Julia Cameron, Head of Communications, IFES (International Fellowship of Evangelical Students)

Expository Thoughts on Genesis

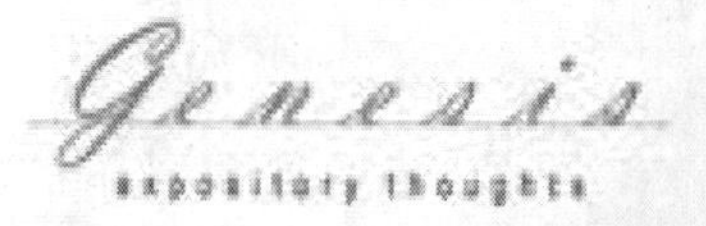

Genesis is the book of beginnings. Here we read of the creation of the world, the creation of human beings, their temptation and fall, the inhabiting of the earth, the destruction of a rebellious world, the lives of the patriarchs, and the great promises of God. Jim Dixon shows us that biblical history is our history, and that Christians living in the twenty-first century need to know the Bible's beginnings.

The sheer size of Genesis makes the book intimidating for many. Expository Thoughts on Genesis will remove the hesitation that many face. The message of Genesis is here presented in devotional segments -bite-size pieces - that inform the heart and instruct the mind. In these pages, Dixon beautifully mines the depths of Genesis and provides answers to a most essential question, How then shall we live?

Jim Dixon is a man who has lived in the text of Genesis and allowed it to harrow his soul. His “Expository Thoughts on Genesis” will cut fresh furrows in the hearts of his readers. The attentive preacher or teacher will find a harvest of expositional inspiration.

– R. Kent Hughes

ISBN 085234 5690

'An Iron Pillar'

The Life and Times of William Romaine

The eighteenth century was fertile ground for the great Evangelical Revival. The lack of morality among the laity and clergy moved many to the pursuit of genuine godliness. William Romaine, an often neglected figure of the period, was one such individual. Through his broad and extensive ministry, Romaine reached thousands for the cause of Christ, calling them to walk deeper paths of holiness.

This biography is more than a bare record of events. It is the story of a Christian who was able to persevere as a shining light in a dark and confusing world. It is the story of a minister, who, though removed by time and culture, still speaks to us today.

ISBN 0 85234 562 3

'If ever we needed "Pillars of Iron" in the church, it is in our own day, when compromise and worldliness are sapping its spiritual power and eroding its influence. May this new biography encourage many, both young preachers and all Christians alike, to be as fearless and faithful for the truth as was William Romaine.'
- Faith Cook

Tim Shenton is also the author of *Christmas Evans, The life and times of the one-eyed preacher of Wales,* and *A Cornish Revival, The life and times of Samuel Walker of Truro*, both published by Evangelical Press. He is the head teacher of St Martin's School and an elder at Lansdowne Baptist Church.

Know Your God

The Doctrine of God in the Pentateuch

Nothing better explains the world in which we live than the fact that modern society is almost totally bereft of the knowledge of God. To make matters worse, the church itself is losing touch with the revelation of God in Holy Scripture. The church does not know her God and many characteristics of modern evangelical life are directly attributable to that ignorance. Nothing is so calculated to enfeeble the church as a diminished or faulty conception of God himself.

In this fine study Linleigh Roberts sets out to reintroduce the church to her God by exploring the revelation of God given in the first five books of the Bible. There is a good reason to begin with the Pentateuch in thinking about God.

Dr Robert Rayburn

Linleigh J. Roberts is an Australian living in the USA. He is a graduate of Moody Bible Institute, Columbia Bible College (now Columbia International University) and Covenant Theological Seminary. In addition to being ordained in the Presbyterian Church in America, he has served for several years as director of Biblical Foundations, International. After teaching in many countries, he is now retired. He is married and has five children and fourteen grandchildren.

ISBN 0 85234 582 8